PRAISE FOR BRILLIANCE

"Our weary spirits have seldom needed this devotional more. An antidote to the fear and uncertainty in our world and hearts, *Brilliance* takes a deep, loving look at the God who longs to be present in our lives. Jane Rubietta shines hope into our soul's dark corners, and offers healing for our pain, timely reminders of how deeply loved we are, and practical ways to allow Christ's love to shine through us. I highly recommend this transformative, six-week journey into finding Christ's light in life's dark seasons."

— LYNN AUSTIN, BESTSELLING AUTHOR
AND CHRISTY HALL OF FAME HONOREE

"Jane Rubietta provides a soothing and challenging voice for today's world with unique insights into the needs of people seeking God. Her fresh approach to scripture couples with a plan for a week of contemplative thought that leads to a weekend of action. Delve into this devotional for a life-changing experience. A book with a verbal hug."

— CLEO LAMPOS, M.ED., SPEAKER,
EDUCATOR, AUTHOR OF *A MOTHER'S SONG*

"*Brilliance* tunnels us through the darkness into light; a delightful and challenging and empowering devotional."

— LYNNE HOWE, WRITER AND ACTIVIST

"Intimate and comforting in a 'let me walk with you' voice, Jane Rubietta's six-week devotional, *Brilliance,* is the faithful friend we need to journey beside us in these uncertain days. Through personal insights into our common struggles, Jane probes scripture, speaks truth, asks quietly challenging questions meant to inspire action and reaches for the loving God who daily showers us with promises and hope. Road-weary when I opened this book, I came away filled. We are deeply, eternally loved, forgiven, redeemed, and designed—even in our imperfect state—to reflect the bright light of God's love. Perfect for reading alone, journaling through or discussing with a group of trusted friends, *Brilliance* is sunrise for the soul."

—CATHY GOHLKE, BESTSELLING AND CHRISTY AWARD-WINNING AUTHOR

BRILLIANCE

Finding Light in Dark Places

JANE RUBIETTA

Abounding Publishing

BRILLIANCE: FINDING LIGHT IN DARK PLACES

copyright ©2020 by Jane Rubietta

Published by Abounding Publishing

Unless otherwise indicated, all scripture quotations are taken from the Holy Bible, New International Version® (NIV), copyright ©1973, 1978, 1984, 2011 by Biblica, Inc.™

Used by permission. All rights reserved worldwide. www.Zondervan.com The "NIV" and "New International Version" are trademarks registered in the United States Patent and Trademark Office by Biblica, Inc.™

Scripture quotations from THE MESSAGE. Copyright © Eugene H. Peterson 1993, 1994, 1995, 1996, 2000, 2001, 2002. Used by Permission of Tyndale House Publishers, Inc.

Scripture quotations marked (ESV) the ESV Bible (The Holy Bible, English Standard Version), copyright © 2001 by Crossway, a publishing ministry of Good News Publishers. Used by Permission. All rights reserved.

Scripture quotations marked (NAS) New American Standard taken from the NEW AMERICAN STANDARD BIBLE, copyright ©1960, 1962, 1963, 1968, 1971, 1972, 1973, 1975 1977, 1995 by The Lockman Foundation. Used by permission.

ISBN-13:978-1-7352414-0-1

Ebook ISBN:978-1-7352414-1-8

❦ Created with Vellum

OTHER TITLES BY JANE RUBIETTA

The Forgotten Life of Evelyn Lewis
Heartbeat of a Mother
Worry Less So You Can Live More
Finding Your Way
Finding Your Promise
Finding Your Name
Finding Your Dream
Finding the Messiah
Finding Life
Come Along
Come Closer
Resting Place
Grace Points
How to Keep the Pastor You Love
Between Two Gardens
Still Waters
Quiet Places

CONTENTS

Introduction	ix
Week One	1
Day One: Job Description	2
Day Two: The Perfect Gift	6
Day Three: Altaring Worry	10
Day Four: Feeding on Demand	14
Day Five: Twirling in Church	18
Weekend One Segue	22
Week Two	25
Day One: Sky-High	26
Day Two: Sighted	30
Day Three: #Fail	34
Day Four: Boots on the Ground	38
Day Five: Training for the High Seas	42
Weekend Two Segue	46
Week Three	49
Day One: Step Out of the Traffic	50
Day Two: The Endless Song	53
Day Three: Rescued from a Red-Light Past	57
Day Four: Klieg Lights	61
Day Five: Saving Lives	65
Weekend Three Segue	68
Week Four	70
Day One: Offstage View	71
Day Two: It's Impossible	74
Day Three: Walking the Line	78
Day Four: Yakety Yak	82
Day Five: Activating Dynamite	86
Weekend Four Segue	90
Week Five	93
Day One: I Once Was Blind	94

Day Two: Looking for Answers	98
Day Three: From Fear to Fasting	102
Day Four: Pack Rat	106
Day Five: Close Encounters of the Healing Kind	110
Weekend Five Segue	114
Week Six	117
Day One: The Bridge	118
Day Two: R.S.V.P and A.S.A.P.	122
Day Three: Thinking Cap	126
Day Four: Thanking You In Advance	130
Day Five: A Table of Misfits	134
Weekend Six Segue	138
Closing Word	141
About Jane Rubietta	143
Notes	145

INTRODUCTION

EVEN THE DARKNESS WILL NOT BE DARK TO YOU;
THE NIGHT WILL SHINE LIKE THE DAY,
FOR DARKNESS IS AS LIGHT TO YOU

PSALM 139:12

At a women's retreat years ago, I lived in a beauty-starved state of soul. Before dawn, I raced outside to catch the sunrise slipping over the horizon and streaming across the lake. Oh, such joy to see the glory of the sun escape the clutches of darkness. Once again, the night did not win!

Later, a retreatant dragged in for the last few seconds of the breakfast buffet, rubbing her eyes. She seemed surprised at the people already awake and ready for the day. We greeted one another, her smile sleepy, mine fully charged.

"I saw the sunrise," I said.

She looked at me with wide eyes, wordless. She blinked, and went into a mini-trance of memory. "I saw the sunrise once."

We laughed. Turns out, not everyone likes dawn, but

aren't we drawn to light? Like so many of us, my friend lived an un-easy life. She found solace and hope outside, her face freckled from gardening, her eyes gleaming with sunshine.

The contrast of light and darkness exists since the beginning of time. Darkness isn't inherently evil—nightfall raises melatonin levels and makes sleep, glorious sleep possible. Night offers healing for body and soul, and sleep often resolves yesterday's remainders of stress and turmoil.

But darkness may remind us of our unknowings, our inabilities, fears, unresolved conflicts, of our backdrop of pain and difficulty. This season may feel more intense than others to you, though our twenty-four-hour periods continue to weave in and out of light and dark, day and night. We need light more than ever. On some level, can't we relate to Isaiah's words?

> "The people walking in darkness have seen a great light; on those living in the land of deep darkness a light has dawned" (9:2).

Light dawns with hope, growth, healing. It heralds the victory of day and the collapse of night. Perhaps this year has held for you an extra measure of grief, or loneliness. Of fear or uncertainty. Unprecedented pain tripped you, or someone you love. Untold losses, soaring economic issues, unemployment, and drastic lifestyle changes occupy and preoccupy the days, and worry the nights. Darkness presses close. But night does not win. Light dawns every single day.

Brilliance leads us through our common denominators of difficulty, loss of vision, and low-tide faith, into the sunrise from on high, the bright morning star, the one who dwells in unapproachable light and in whom are no shifting shadows.

As the Psalmist so beautifully phrased it,

> If I rise on the wings of the dawn,
>> if I settle on the far side of the sea,
> even there your hand will guide me,
>> your right hand will hold me fast.
> If I say, "Surely the darkness will hide me
>> and the light become night around me,"
> even the darkness will not be dark to you;
>> the night will shine like the day,
>> for darkness is as light to you
> (Psalm 139:9-12).

Literally nowhere can we flee, but that God meets us. No darkness is too thick to render God's light and presence impotent.

The hope of Christ's bright presence in our everyday fumbling and bumbling, the comfort of the Holy Spirit during times of isolation and loneliness, the truth of scripture: these are normal staples for our Christian life. However, when life feels dark and so many of the structures in our life are compromised or obliterated, those standard certainties can feel irrelevant or even trite.

With so many changes, a soul-companion can be the best way through the day, so we aren't attempting to navigate our lives by ourselves. My hope, with these daily writings, is to come alongside one another in our everyday-ness, so that neither of us is alone during this time. Whether the days fill with crushing duties or the calendar stares back with blank eyes, this selection of readings can steady our day, or refuel our lunch break, or tuck us into bed at night.

Each day includes a scripture to mull over, and a short devotional, along with some questions for reflection and journaling. The reading closes with a prayer for application. The daily layout makes for easy facilitation in a small group.

The weekend offerings vary. A few thoughts to ponder,

questions to consider, or other relevant tools to bridge us over from one week to the next. Although I love learning about scripture, delving into original language words and meaning, it's easy to halt with learning. More than just information, scripture is a powerful tool for transformation. Thus, each weekend gathers the week's five verses, providing a chance to meditate on them. This is an old tool from the saints called *Lectio Divina,* meaning divine or sacred reading, and leads to experiencing God's presence in a way that is both applicable and transformative.

Even if you don't currently journal, you might consider a notebook to keep track of your soul's progress, what God speaks into you, where the Holy Spirit comforts or challenges you. That's a safe place to respond to the reflection questions, as well. Since it is not good to be alone incessantly, this book is also designed for groups, whether online or phone or face-to-face.

Life is a day-in, day-out journey interwoven with dark and light, sun and shadow. May we find God there, and find ourselves loved. Because that is the most vital truth of our day, every single day of our lives. We are deeply loved.

That kind of truth changes the way we live. That kind of love changes the world. Yours. Mine. And the great yonder. Talk about brilliance.

WEEK ONE

DAY ONE: JOB DESCRIPTION

LET'S GET TO WORK

> "THE LIGHT SHINES IN THE DARKNESS, AND THE DARKNESS
> HAS NOT OVERCOME IT."
> JOHN 1:5

A blind man, begging by the side of the road? Talk about darkness: he lived in a land without light. But darkness, too, of people. Mocked, belittled. Bartimaeus couldn't even see the kicks coming, couldn't dodge the fists, let alone the jeers, the jokes, the bullying. How this son of Timaeus—meaning "precious" in Greek—sat rattling his tin can in the dirt we don't know. Don't know what happened to his family, nothing. Only that he experienced firsthand a world of darkness.[1] (See Mark 10:46-52.)

With the news that Jesus passed by, hope beat a bass drum in his chest. The man who heals! Bartimaeus shouted,

"Jesus, son of David, have mercy on me!" Who could blame him?

Well, plenty of people. In fact, they rebuked and shushed him. "No wounds allowed. Buck up. Put on a parade face so we look good in the cover photos." Imagine the headline: Happy Blind Man Cheers Jesus On.

Too late for shushing. This man had begged a thousand begs. He knew exactly what he wanted, and shouted even louder, "Son of David, have mercy on me!" When Jesus called to him, Bartimaeus flung aside his cloak and leapt to his feet, sensing his way to Jesus.

"What do you want me to do for you?" the rabbi asked.

"I want to see." There. He'd said it, stated the obvious, dared to spell out in bold font the ridiculous longing of his soul. He couldn't see people's reactions, but the hairs on his arms stood out, antennae of awareness. The scorn and disbelief and then their snorting at his stupidity.

But Jesus' words would change his darkness into light: "Go. Your faith has healed you" (v. 52).

Imagine, when light and sight poured in, him blinking in the brilliance of a color-wheeling world. Imagine the fireworks of wonder, and his soul-recognition as he saw the man's face who'd spoken light into the dark. No wonder Bartimaeus followed on Jesus' heels clear to Jerusalem. And what he saw on the route! How it must have brightened his soul, the sights now providing images for the soundscape of his life.

Then, just when he thought light was there to stay, Bartimaeus saw with his own eyes the truth of people's darkness, the sin-blinded, hate-darkened, clench-fisted lives of those who would trade this good man's life for a criminal's. He watched soldiers pound spikes into his Healer's wrists and ankles, then hoist the cross into the air. Saw the light and life drain away.

The crushing nighttime returned. Darkness fell over the

entire earth, a lifetime of darkness poured into three hours of daylight, collapsing the fragile light of hope.

So much for Isaiah's prophecy: "The people walking in darkness have seen a great light" (9:2). On Good Friday, that day of horrors and broken dreams and no apparent goodness, on that day when evil seemed to triumph, darkness fell over all the earth.

How to reconcile Friday's dark shadows, juxtaposed with the One about whom John said, "In him was life, and that life was the light of all"? And that "The light shines in the darkness, and the darkness has not overcome it" (1:4-5)?

In a world still dwelling in darkness, in our own lives with their intermittent shadows and the gloom of disappointment, pain, grief, and death, the light still lives. Because Friday's light-quenching black hole is no longer the whole story. On Saturday, while Bartimaeus reeled from this fresh darkness, and Mary grieved the death of her perfect child, and the disciples locked themselves in fear in that Upper Room, Jesus cleaned house in hell. The next morning, darkness collapsed in the brilliant light of resurrection. Death died, and light won.

"What do you want me to do for you?" Jesus had asked. Bartimaeus defined the mercy he sought: "I want to see." This season, let's name our mercy.

I want to see. To see dawn though night reigns, to see darkness die in me and light grow. To bring the unconquerable light into the darkness of the world, so others can see.

Sounds like a job for the Light of the World.

Just Wondering...

THERE ARE mile markers for most of us, memories pinned to

the top of our life page. Dates, or experiences. A moment when our life pivoted, a dramatic or drastic event occurred. Perhaps it is darkness. Maybe it's light. What are some of yours? How did your life change as a result?

WITHOUT STOPPING to ponder whether your answer feels spiritual enough, hear Jesus ask you: "What do you want me to do for you?" Answer quickly and honestly. Then really tell Jesus that.

WHAT DARKNESS in you needs to die? Where do you need light today?

Dear Jesus,
Thank you for bringing light, for being Light.
Fill me with your light,
and help light grow in the world through me.
Amen.

DAY TWO: THE PERFECT GIFT

THE NESTLING HOPE

"Every good and perfect gift is from above."
James 1:17

One year, we observed the Twelve Days of Birthday, the climax being the party for 35 close friends, held on our lawn, just at the eve of the season. Our yard was off the mosquito map, the nearby lake bracingly cool for watermelon football, and life was good. Unfortunately, as in a novel, the birthday morning, the real birthday at last, created a bit of a denouement for our birthday honoree.[1]

In the midst of wrapping paper torn and scattered across the dining room, tissue paper wadded as from the fists of a blocked writer, it became obvious, to my closely watching gaze at least, that the gifts were a disappointment. Nothing exactly right: wrong color, or size, or taste. Total misfits, these gifts did not fulfill the anticipation created by the occasion and wrapping and hoopla. Nor did they satisfy the hope snuggling quietly alongside the sadness, watching the celebration with alert eyes.

This secret sadness skulks behind so many special events: a birthday breakfast or anniversary dinner or Valentine's Day or Christmas present-fest. The not-quite sweater, the almost-blouse, the default tie, the totally-off tech gadget, the who-could-even-think-of-it appliance, the complete miss wall art or car widget. These leave a residue of tiny grief at not being well-known enough in our core self, not being well-loved enough, for another to find the perfect gift.

Doesn't that God-given sadness spring from a nestling hope? How normal to hope for the perfect gift, the delightful surprise—to want someone to understand the longings of our heart that we can't express or scrawl on a wish list or dream of in a present. Birthdays, Christmas, and anniversaries take us to that place of hope and dream—of a love that knows us so deeply, our wordless desires intimately known to this perfect friend or family member or lover.

We so badly want someone to love us by divining the perfect present, this perfect gift that says, "You are 100% loved because you are 100% known and accepted. I knew exactly what that perfect gift would be."

We want a loved one who keeps delighting us by expressing perfect love through a surprising package. It's "The Wells Fargo Wagon" and *Music Man* day after day, year after year.

But in reality, will we always be left, after recycling the gift wrap and collapsing the boxes, with that twinge of disappointment, that flick of sorrow crouched behind bright eyes and strong hugs and effusive thank yous? In truth, this deeply-knowing kind of gift-giving only comes from one place, the Giver of every good and perfect gift.

So, like someone awaiting mail, I resolve to watch; for that sneaking sadness, that longing for perfect that subtly creeps into my soul and relationships, that can only be satisfied by the One who created it in the first place. Today, I resolve to redirect that longing to its Giver, and to watch for the perfect gifts.

Starting now, I'm keeping track. So far, today, the tally shows a besotted Lover, offering a delightful variety of perfect gifts. The perfect sunrise—bouncing up from the horizon, bouncing off the nearby lake, bouncing into our bedroom at 5:16 this morning, like a child bouncing on the bed. "Wake up! See what I've done just for you! Look at this beauty...just for you."

The perfect cup of coffee—is there anything so smooth, so perfectly warming and satisfying, as the very first cup, steaming, strong, a dollop of cream, first thing after a sunrise wakeup?

Now, a perfect gentle soaking rain, watering the thirsty trees and grass (and I just mowed yesterday—how's that for another perfect-timing gift?), and the silence that attends the rain as gentle as a lady in waiting. Muting of the traffic, quieting of the wildlife. "*Shh, shh*," says this perfect gift. "Rest awhile."

And sometimes, the perfect gift comes wrapped in unexpected paper: perhaps pain. Like the words someone shared with me with over the weekend, prompting first anger, then pain, and then soul-searching to delve to the bottom of the package that will ultimately make me a more whole human being. Not a bad gift to offer the people around me.

With gifts like this, who wants only Twelve Days of Birthday? I'll take 365, please, all in a row. Year after year until at last I meet the Perfect Gift face to face, and hope is turned to sight, the secret sadness banished in the brilliance.

Until then, I'll be at my post. Watching and celebrating.

. . .

Just Wondering...

When do you long for a special something—anything!—that shows you are deeply known and treasured?

How does that longing appear? When has the gift, in fact, been perfect?

What perfect gifts from God are you seeing in this day?

Dear God,
Only in you is my longing for perfect love satisfied.
Fill me with that love, that I might love more wholly,
and live more holy, in Jesus' name.
Amen.

DAY THREE: ALTARING WORRY

THE MOST IMPORTANT CALL

> "The Lord will fight for you;
> you need only to be still."
> Exodus 14:14

After deciding to initiate a difficult discussion that affected both my personal and professional wellbeing, I jittered about my office. I anticipated this with all the joy of a patient heading into surgery without anesthesia. I don't do conflict well, and always feel red-faced and incoherent. Preoccupation rendered me nearly ineffective at my desk. As the day waned, my anxiety level increased. The list of items to address in a conversation I hadn't started parked its eighteen-wheeler on my chest.[1]

People-pleasing ways rose up in chattering insecurity, my heart practically fibrillating in worry. The possibility of alienating a colleague nittered and nipped at my soul, a tiny barking anxious dog.

For context, my office is a converted chapel; the altar remains at one end of the narrow room. I moved in with a monstrous workload and abandoned boxes still cluttered both sides of the altar. Once a friend peered around the piles and observed, "Some days I really need an altar."

On the day of conflict—or maybe, really, it was about communication rather than conflict, a pileup of missed and misunderstood messages that needed to be decoded—I reviewed my list. Tried to pray. Jittered some more.

The dish-clattering in my soul was like a neglected wife slamming about the kitchen in hopes of being noticed. Into that din, the altar called to me, this inaudible but clear beckoning. Surprised, I looked over at the gleaming walnut backdrop. Without a second thought, I obeyed. My legs took me to the altar, and I folded myself there on the floor.

I exhaled. Inhaled. Repeated. And at last prayed.

Hunched on the floor, shoulders tense, legs crunched, I waited, unable to rise. The work of the altar was just beginning. Into the wait sounded one thin line, clear and fleeting as a voice on the telephone. "The Lord your God fights for you."

My heart shot off fireworks. But still I waited.

"You need only to be still."

I raised my head, puzzled. Well, didn't I still need to make the phone call? I still needed to have the conversation, didn't I?

Of course. Crawling to my feet, I grabbed my phone. The person picked up on the first ring. "Jane? Where are you? Are you in your office? I'm standing outside your door."

Even now, my eyes widen and I shake my head. God brought the person to my office door? In this remote building, on the third floor?

Isn't worry about the future, rather than this present split-second in time? We worry in present tense, tense about the future, projecting our fear across the windshield separating us from tomorrow. Worry is about wellbeing, ours or another's or the world's.

After the conversation—which never felt conflictual, and ended on a friendly note of understanding and cooperation—I returned to my office. The altar presided at the south end, dark wood shining.

And then I noticed the three carvings on the wall piece. On one side, the Alpha. On the other side, the Omega. Two Greek letters, meaning the Beginning and the End.

In the middle, a Latin symbol, an X with a P in the center. The peace of Christ.

Christ the Beginning, Christ the End, Christ the peace in between.

Maybe tomorrow, I can start there, at the altar, with Christ who knows the end from the beginning, and offers peace in between. What is there, after all, to worry about?

Just Wondering...

What's your current anxious, barking dog that nitters at your soul?

How do you typically experience worry? And how do you react to it?

Be still, and let Moses' words to the Israelites sink in. "The Lord will fight for you." Wait with that promise. What do you need to *do*, then, in response?

Dear God,
It's easier to worry than to wait in your presence.
But you promise me your peace, and that you fight for me.
Help me to be still,
so that all my living comes from your presence in me.
Amen.

DAY FOUR: FEEDING ON DEMAND

FOOD FOR THE SOUL

> "Look at the birds of the air; they do not sow or
> reap or store away in barns,
> and yet your heavenly Father feeds them.
> Are you not much more valuable than they?"
> Matthew 6:26

The baby birds outside my window insist. No, in their tiny voices out of their megaphone beaks, they demand to be fed. "I'm starving, my miniature tummy holds so little food, I'm ravenous all day and we have a lot of catching up to do after a long silent night. Feed me, feed me, feed me some more."

Their mouths open so wide, opera singers should take note. Those beaks practically form a flat diamond shape as the babies sing for their supper, breakfast, lunch, and nonstop snacks in between. These midgets stick their heads through the holes in the ramshackle birdhouse as soon as they hear a parent approaching. However, they don't actually sing, not yet: they project demanding notes, honest sounds about their deepest needs. This is how they stay alive.

I wonder about that, about what is lost in our self-deprecating society, in our world where no one has needs and certainly no one talks about them. Today, I sat with Bible and journal and decaf coffee and chocolate and invited myself into God's presence. I wrote a few words, didn't open the scriptures, guzzled my coffee and chocolate chips, and finally just sat.

What would my heart-cry be, if like the baby birds I open my mouth to project it to God? What would yours sound like? Would anyone be around to listen to it? If food is one of our basic necessities on Maslow's hierarchy, where does it fit into your pyramid? Not your coffee and chocolate or bacon and eggs, but the spiritual food, without which you die of starvation?

I wake up hungry: hungry for God, for stillness, for beauty. But I'm noticing that this dawn feeding doesn't last much past the world's wake-up call, and something needs to change about my nurture schedule. The baby birds literally eat all day long, every time the parent birds appear at the entrance to their tenement housing with its absentee landlord. (The basement is falling out of this little house, and all the bird-parents moved their families to the upper story.)

Just so, God is an attentive parent, knowing perfectly well our deep need for holy presence. How I love it that the Holy Spirit is depicted at Jesus' baptism as a dove—a bird! And part of the Holy Spirit's role is to comfort, counsel, convict, guide us into truth. In other words, to nurture us. What will it look like, then, all day, every day, to open my mouth to God's feeding, to proclaim my deepest needs?

Listening to my tummy, or more accurately, my peeping heart, first of all. What do I need? Yesterday, I needed some soothing after an angry phone conversation (my anger, unfortunately): *"Shhh, shhh, what about that upset you, baby bird?"* I had to wait with my rampant blood pressure to listen into my soul, past the anger, to the longing to be heard. Opening my mouth to God meant directing that longing to heaven, asking forgiveness for not listening sooner, for hurting another, and waiting for a few minutes to be loved and tended.

Maybe in this feeding-on-demand schedule, we consciously pull in a deep breath of God's presence, filling up with the Holy Spirit, a spiritual high-carb energy supplement mid-workout. When the cacophony of the world or my own clanging irritabilities overwhelms me, just thirty seconds at my desk with my mouth shut clears my mind, releases my radioactive anxiety, refocuses my soul.

A prayer before placing a phone call feeds my chirping heart. Sometimes, I just ask, "God, please bring your word to mind." Wherever we are, whatever we are doing, mid-flight or stationary in our ramshackle little buildings that are our bodies, God waits to feed us, like a dove alighting with a beak-full of sustenance.

It's pretty simple, really. Just listen to your baby-bird heart, and open your mouth. *Bon appétit!*

Just Wondering...

WHAT DO you usually feel hungry for? Do you fall into one of these two camps: eat to live? Or live to eat?

. . .

How does your soul hunger manifest? When do you notice it?

Pick one means of redirecting your heart to God throughout the day that will nourish your soul. What is it? How will you use that method? (So many options. Some to consider: silence, a chorus or hymn, deep breaths, raising your hands toward God, standing at a window looking for birds...)

Dear God,
Thank you for hunger that reminds me of your faithfulness.
Help me to recognize and bring my hunger to you,
that you might feed me throughout the day.
Amen.

DAY FIVE: TWIRLING IN CHURCH

ENCIRCLED BY LOVE

"Rejoice with those who rejoice."
Romans 12:15

She was an impish brunette and six years old. We met at a wedding, and later at church. There, after the service, several of us clustered in a group, I the only mother with grown children. The other moms still have birds in the nest, some of them scarcely with feathers, let alone flying and sometimes free-falling.[1]

This little elf planted herself in the center of the adult women, smiling. She started twirling in a circle between us, a ballerina practicing her turns. Her mother tried to still her, and the child covered her face by putting her hood on backwards, then spinning some more.

"Stop twirling," her mother said. "You will fall down."

I wondered about that, whether the mother was really worried about her child falling, or about her becoming the center of attention, or disturbing the peace. Would the child really fall down, this little girl so much closer to the ground, so much more centered, than we were? Than we are, we wise adult women who want so much to control our worlds and not have our children make us—*ahem*—look bad in the process.

One mistake I have made, as a mother, has been attempting to control my children in case they disturbed others, when they were only being children, doing childlike stuff. Like spinning into adult conversations that are stiflingly boring to a kid needing to know she, too, exists in a circle of women.

"Why don't you see what happens if you keep spinning?" I suggested. I, the new adult to the group. I'm recognizing, belatedly, the wisdom of allowing kids to find their limits in safety, with small decisions and small consequences, than to wait until they fling from the coop and crash in a big way. Twirling in church in a circle of women seemed a safe experiment with risk and safety.

"No, don't listen to Mrs. Rubietta. I want you to stop spinning," her mother said.

Appalled, I realized I'd trespassed her authority. I wasn't the child's mother or even her mother's friend, and had no business (or intention) suggesting anarchy.

"Please listen to your mother, honey," I said, a tad late noticing the context. And to the mother, "Please forgive me. I didn't mean to suggest disobedience or usurp your authority."

Plus, I didn't know the full story. Though she behaved like an angel throughout the church service, maybe the child spun out of control daily and her mother constantly had to reel her in, wind her back up into the nest. Maybe at six the child had such a twirling streak that she couldn't ever sit still, couldn't stop long enough to listen or learn, to help, to be part of the life around her.

But later, I felt sad, sad for the little girl who couldn't twirl in church. One of the gifts we can give, as adults in the Body of Christ, is acceptance and the ability to be childlike. I can't imagine a safer place to spin, in a sanctuary and right inside a circle of women who love you and think you adorable. I so hope she can find spinning places, to experience the dizzying delight of childlikeness, the joy of a world that circles you, if only for a moment. And arms to catch you when—not if, but when—you fall.

Somehow, I think Jesus would smile if he caught us twirling in church, twirling for the sake of sheer joy, because we're alive and so is he. And he'd catch us if we fell, stand us back up on our feet.

I want to be that kind of a Christ-follower, delighting in others' differences even if those differences create a little bit of commotion. And who knows? One day, maybe I'll even twirl.

Just Wondering...

Our kids used to regularly get chastised by well-meaning church members for being too active (as in, running) in church. What rules did you have for movement in church?

When have you experienced judgement for twirling kind of behavior?

. . .

How about safety? Who are the safe people who encircle you and allow you to experiment with moving forward in your life?

Where do you struggle to appreciate others' differences? How can you shift toward acceptance and encouragement?

Dear God,
You tell me that you spin with joy over me, in Zephaniah 3:17.
Help me to rejoice over others, even if it isn't convenient.
In your presence, we can safely spin.
Amen!

WEEKEND ONE SEGUE

Weekends can open up all sorts of opportunities for accelerated growth and application, although in my experience they tend to create their own long list of catch-up and to-dos that must happen right now if not sooner. Saturdays in particular have high expectations: make people happy, attend to emotional needs from the week that got ignored, clean the entire house, run errands, throw in a load of laundry, take Junior 1 to practice, Junior 2 to babysit, Senior 1 on an adventure, move the laundry over, phone or text or video-chat with people you've missed all week, forget you needed to feed people, do another load of laundry, strip the beds you forgot to change last week, or last month. Remember you needed to feed someone, possibly yourself, and throw some crumbs into the nearest complaining belly.

Then we skid into Sunday, and we're panting and desperate and also feeling like abject failures for being so snippy, hasty, and messy on Saturday. We crawl on hot coals to church, if we're able, repent in dust and ashes and rend our clothes. Or, just feel really isolated and disconnected, with lots of #fail thrown in.

How about, this weekend, if you soak up one of the passages from the week?

Here is the week's list:

"The light shines in the darkness, and the darkness has not overcome it."
John 1:5

"Every good and perfect gift is from above."
James 1:17

"The Lord will fight for you; you need only to be still."
Exodus 14:14

"Look at the birds of the air; they do not sow or reap or store away in barns, and yet your heavenly Father feeds them. Are you not much more valuable than they?"
Matthew 6:26

"Rejoice with those who rejoice."
Romans 12:15

READ OVER THE LIST SLOWLY, and invite the Holy Spirit to speak to you through one in particular.

Now, read that one tiny verse slowly. Then, wait. Let the words sink into your soul. Is there something God is highlighting for you? A word, or phrase, or challenge?

Next, ask, "What? What would you have me to do, God?" And listen for the answer.

REPEAT this process several times with the verse. Consider writing the "What" answer on a 3x5 card, and carrying it with you to apply throughout the day.

WEEK TWO

DAY ONE: SKY-HIGH

AN INCONVENIENT PERSPECTIVE

> "AS THE HEAVENS ARE HIGHER THAN THE EARTH,
> SO ARE MY WAYS HIGHER THAN YOUR WAYS
> AND MY THOUGHTS THAN YOUR THOUGHTS."
> ISAIAH 55:9

The 737 dilly-dallied outside the gate at O'Hare, victim of some sort of computer glitch. We dozed, we sweated, we talked on our phones. Ninety minutes late, we lifted into the not-so-friendly skies (given some semi-irate passengers) and the nose of the plane turned westward for our four-hour trip across America.

Personally, I was really in a hurry. I'd been a grandmother for exactly five days, and was in a dying tear to get to California for a business trip and then to help this tiny exhausted family and meet our brand-new baby, the first grandchild on all sides. I hadn't stopped smiling for 120 hours, or pacing, or packing or phoning, and sending texts and pictures and staring at that beautiful never-before-created face.

Somewhere over the Rocky Mountains, the loudspeaker crackled and the pilot greeted us. Aware, it seems, of his disgruntled patrons, he began reeling off some statistics. We left Chicago with 45,000 pounds of fuel in a $70 million airplane, and were flying at 522 mph, at 77 percent the speed of sound. Beyond our metal, winged bullet, the temperature dropped to -70 degrees Fahrenheit. By then, we had burned about 19,800 pounds, or 2900 gallons, of jet fuel, with an average fuel economy of 12.4 gallons per minute. He spilled out more stats, a ticker tape I couldn't catch: the gallons of gas and hours burned driving cross-country, multiplied by the two hundred passengers onboard, and how frequently cars have accidents. His bottom line: the total efficiency of air travel, with or without a slow start at the gate.

Outside my 12" by 12" window, the glory of the earth below spread in radiant splendor. The deep gorge of the Grand Canyon, with its layers of color and shading, the spackling of snow on the mountains. Before Orville and Wilbur, the Wright brothers, this sight and perspective were visible only to birds and to God. Now we mortals soared above it. What did it matter if we were a little, or even a lot, late lifting off? We had seat-belted ourselves into a veritable miracle, this silver sleek jet conveying us to the shores of the Pacific Ocean.

From this vantage point, I imagined our ancestors waving off their children as the wagons headed west, and possibly never heard from or saw them again, never met and held and hugged and bonded with their grandbabies. From this vantage point, I considered God's point of view: the certainty that our Alpha and Omega, the One who is past, present and future the same, knows the beginning from the end because Jesus is already there.

This same God knows exactly when we need to be anywhere.

> "As the heavens are higher than the earth,
>   so are my ways higher than your ways
>   and my thoughts than your thoughts"
> (Isaiah 55:9).

We take our conveniences for granted, and our inconveniences irk and anger us. Shall I really complain over a delay brief in light of eternity past and future? All the irritations of our lives, viewed from above the firmament, are but a single pixel in the big picture. They matter so little compared to the relationships around us and the joy of serving God, the privilege of seeing God do what we cannot possibly do on our own. Seeing what God does that we cannot even imagine, let alone create.

When the flight's captain rattled off the facts of our jet-set travel, the gentleman in the seat next to me leaned over. "Sounds like he's doing some damage control."

No doubt. Sometimes, we just need the Pilot's sky-high perspective. Like the vista outside our plane, six miles up in the air.

Just Wondering...

When do inconveniences irk you? How do you gain perspective?

. . .

How do you feel about damage control? Yours, or someone else's? How do you respond, for instance, when someone is trying to spin a situation to try to help you feel better?

How do you shift from your own perspective (for example: I'm late, this stinks, no one cares, I'm in charge and blowing it) to God's? When have you experienced God's viewpoint in such a way that it truly does change your approach to a situation?

*Dear God,
I'm so thankful that your thoughts are higher than mine!
What a relief. Help me to see life, people,
and problems from your perspective today.
Amen.*

DAY TWO: SIGHTED

SEEN AND LOVED

> "WHEN JESUS LANDED AND SAW A LARGE CROWD,
> HE HAD COMPASSION ON THEM AND HEALED THEIR SICK."
> MATTHEW 14:14

People, wearing sweatshirts and work clothes and fancy sandals and dress-to-impress threads, jam the trendy coffee spot. To connect, to work, to snag a relationship. Some probably come for coffee.[1]

Tucked along the wall, father and son stare, unblinking, at their phones. Dad's second phone rests on the table in front of him, just in case. In case of what, an organ transplant? The boy slips down on the padded bench until his spine suspends him almost over the edge of the seat. They gulped their drinks and ate their treats and now disappear into a techno-daze.

The daughter watches them, and the mass of chattery people, through thick glasses. A green straw glued to her lips delivers sweet empty calories in a steady stream. She swings her leg. When she glances down, stringy hair blocks her face. That straight hair and lonely countenance remind me of every child, abandoned in a crowd of loud that doesn't even acknowledge her.

How will their lives go? Indeed, how will anyone's life take shape after being so thoroughly molded by the isolating technology of the communications industry? (A stretch, to imagine this particular tool as one of true communication.) How do we begin to talk to one another, or understand who we are apart from the devices in our hands? If no one meets our eyes, do we even exist?

Perhaps it's not a new question or issue. When Adam and Eve opened their surprised new eyes, they found God, staring them in the face, every inch the delighted parent. Maybe we've been hoping to see God every time we open our own eyes. Years after the First Couple, we witness this longing in people shoving toward a man known as Healer. The crowds rush headlong in their anonymity toward hope.

Jesus has just received notice of John's brutal beheading. Even as he processes his grief and horror (how could he not grieve this man's death, the man who baptized him in the Jordan River, the cousin who recognized Jesus in the womb and somersaulted with joy?), his own pain doesn't cloud his vision or his calling.

The scriptures tell us, "When Jesus landed and saw a large crowd, he had compassion on them and healed their sick" (Matt. 14:14). He sees, really notices, the mass of people clamoring for help.

But he doesn't just see them. Compassion, a word used only of Jesus in the New Testament, filled him. Compassion for the diseased, the sick, the blind, the leprous. Compassion in the Greek means from the innermost parts, from the intestines—something so core and elemental that it wells up and spills over in Jesus' presence, touch, healing. A tender merciful love that recognizes another's suffering and suffers alongside. Jesus feels it in his gut. And then he heals them.

We place ourselves in the midst of the melee. Their cries verbalize our own longings: to be seen, to be cared for, to be healed, to be free of fear and abandonment and loneliness and grief. Imagine Jesus, reeling from grief. He meets your eyes. *Your* eyes. He sees you, truly recognizes that you are his, *you* are the very reason he plunged to earth. You, right there, with one hand clutching empty air and the other pressing on your chest as though to hold in the pain. You, sucking on a straw that delivers a feel-good rush but then just adds a bloated emptiness. You, with your gaze desperately searching faces for someone who notices you.

You. You are seen. Seen, and loved.

Now it's our turn. I glance again at the lonely child on the bench, staring at people blind to her presence. Little one, God sees you. I see you. And pray that you'll know you are seen, and loved, not for what you do or how you look. You are Jesus' focus.

Here's looking at you.

JUST WONDERING...

WHEN DO YOU FEEL IGNORED, or invisible? How often?

WHAT DO you make of the word compassion, being used only of Jesus in the New Testament? How does that fact speak to you?

. . .

Who has seen you, really seen you, and spoken love into you through eye contact? How can you experience eye contact with Jesus?

Dear Jesus,
Open my eyes to see your love.
And then, please fill me to share your love with others.
Help me to see, really see, people today.
Amen.

DAY THREE: #FAIL

ONE GOOD TURN

"AND WHEN YOU HAVE TURNED, STRENGTHEN" THE OTHERS.
LUKE 22:32

"This is my story. This is my song." In two languages, four hundred Hmong friends sang Fanny Crosby's "Blessed Assurance." These families fled to North America for refuge from persecution. Their lives heralded a story of a great God, great hardship, and great faith.[1]

Remember Peter, before Jesus' arrest? Jesus had said, "Satan has asked permission to sift you as wheat. I have prayed for you, that your faith may not fail. When you have turned, strengthen the others." (See Luke 22:14-33.)

Peter's reaction? "I'll never deny you. I'll go with you into death."

Jesus knew better. Within hours, Peter denied three times

even knowing Jesus, let alone loving this man he'd trailed for three years. Peter, and the other disciples with him, failed. Feared. Fled. They locked themselves away, where one night, Peter said, brilliantly, "Let's go fishing" (John 21:1-13).

Fishing? Didn't they *leave* those nets to follow Jesus?

Right. That life segment ended badly. Plan B shifted into Plan A, and off they trundled, shook out their nets, cast into the waters. One long dark night, in a rocking boat. Nothing worked. Not the past, not their present. Empty of fish, filled with failure, weighted with betrayal and loss. These former fishermen fished. All. Night. And caught nothing. Zip. Zilch. Nada.

Plan B. #Fail. Plan A. #Fail. Now what?

When the sun rose, a man stood, silhouetted by shadow. "Haven't you any fish?"

Busted. More #Fail.

But wait. At the man's command, the washed-up fishermen again threw in their nets, hauling in such a huge mess of fish it made history. There on the beach, Jesus invited Peter et al to breakfast, into relationship, into forgiveness, into calling. There, Peter's song and story changed.

Unless we know the backstory, his future successes—thousands of people added to the church! Passion, death threats, courage, conversions—are all overwhelming and unattainable for the general public. Only the superstars, the #Success people, experience such astounding triumph.

Not true. Peter's accomplishments are most meaningful in context of his greatest failure.

The if-onlies of failure riddle all our lives. If only I hadn't made that mistake, failed in that relationship, dropped that ball, betrayed that person. If only.

Failure became part of Peter's story—the part that gave him credibility to "strengthen the others." Without the context of failure, forgiveness is not applicable. What's to forgive? Resurrection means nothing. Breakfast on the beach, that miracle of sustenance and provision, is just a nice picnic.

Without the #Fail, who could relate? But because of that, others witnessed the power of Christ in Peter. Through him. Transformed from someone who feared, failed, fled—into someone inviting people to "declare the praises of him who called you out of darkness into his wonderful light" (I Peter 2:9).

#Fail. A great common denominator among all who dress in earthly skin and bones. But when failure leads to forgiveness, to a turning point over a charcoal fire at sunrise, when we deserve nothing, nothing—well, our stories offer others hope.

What's your story, what's your song? Your past imperfects, your present forgiveness? Where have you failed, been found, been forgiven?

"I have prayed for you"—not that you will not fail. Because you will. "I have prayed for you, that your faith will not fail. And when you have turned, strengthen the others."

#Fail. #Success. The ultimate turnaround.

Turns out, we are super qualified. And that story will sing.

Just Wondering...

What would you say about yourself, if you were to write three sentences to the statement: "This is my story, this is my song"?

When does #fail seem more of your own story, than #success? In what areas do you primarily feel a failure?

. . .

"When you have turned," Jesus said. What were some turning points for you?

How have you found the #fail episodes or seasons becoming means of strengthening others?

Dear God,
Thank you for your forgiveness. Although, that business about failure is not exactly my favorite melody line.
I'd love to tell any story except the ones of my failures.
Please show me how to strengthen others on their #fail journeys.
Amen.

DAY FOUR: BOOTS ON THE GROUND

POLISHING A WORN-OUT SOUL

> "STAND FIRM THEN...WITH YOUR FEET FITTED WITH THE READINESS
> THAT COMES FROM THE GOSPEL OF PEACE."
> EPHESIANS 6:14-15

"Boots, Lady. Come get those boots shined here." His rich voice cut through the airport hubbub.[1]

I skimmed a glance at my scuffed, poor-excuse-for-leather-care footwear. With a million miles of movement, hand-me-downs from my daughter, these boots are made for walking and their re-soling proves it.

After recent breaks in both my foot and ankle, boots are my go-to shoe. Maybe it *would* help if they didn't look quite so downtrodden. I paused mid-airport aisle. To respond to this man's shoeshine call would be momentous. Only three people have ever polished my shoes, except for my own rare and messy attempts: my father, my husband, and once, a polishing man at O'Hare.

I wheeled briefcase and self over to this gentleman, whose resplendent grin outshone the Saint Louis sunshine. "We'll have you all shined up." With a spritz of a cloth, his interested patter began. "How was your holiday?"

"Just great." (Truth? It was hard, our first with my parents both in heaven, but we made it through.) "And yours?"

We chatted—favorite holiday foods, generations-old family recipes—and all the while he worked my road-weary boots. "How long you been at this?" I asked.

Forty years, turns out.

"Full time?"

His laugh flowed, melted chocolate. "My real passion is preaching the Good News. I can't get enough words out about the goodness of God," he said. Now my smile surely lit the airport. We high-fived, and he waxed as eloquent as the emerging luster on my boots.

My partial truth about our holiday stung my soul. Internally, I had been nearly prostrate with grief. Weariness kept me awake at night, a soul fatigue unexpected. The Holy Spirit pulled me through a zillion miles of ministry in the midst of the season of loss, but my soul no longer glowed. Not like his. A worn-out soul. My journal reflected this strange, non-emotive place. Scripture seemed flat, church hollow. My mind either wandered or I dozed during prayer or silence. Only by God's help did we muscle through.

The cloths slipped over the black leather, movements practiced until perfected. Spritz. Clean. Polish. Rub. *Snap.* Repeat.

Spritz.
Clean.
Repeat.

Polish.
Rub.
Buff.
Snap.
Repeat.

And as he worked his craft, my new friend preached, his voice music to my heart. His journey to Jesus, the rivers of faith tradition that deepened him, and his newfound landing at a place of grace.

His work—and didn't he live St. Paul's words, "Whatever you do, work at it with all your heart...as for the Lord, not for men"?—and his words moved me deeply. We shook hands, Philip and I, and I wheeled my briefcase to my gate. Every step, my feet reflected light.

Nestled into the small plane, I opened my Bible. Familiar words shimmered with a new sheen. God filled me in that window seat. For the first time in weeks, tears flooded at the wonder of God's care, these living words warming my soul.

Like the Philip who time-traveled to the Ethiopian eunuch, this Philip met me in my travels, my road weary state, and spilled forth the glory of the good news.

Philip lived it. Just one man, doing his job. Whole-heartedly. Boots on the ground, as they say.

I noticed my boots again as I deplaned. Blessed are the feet. The hands. And the words of those who bring the Good News. May we bring it on, with all our hearts.

Just Wondering...

EVERYONE HAS DOWNTRODDEN MOMENTS. Or days, weeks, months. When are some of yours? What led you into that place?

. . .

WHO HAS INVITED you into "soul polishing," reminding you of joy and hope? How did that help?

HOW WOULD YOU DEFINE "GOOD NEWS" in terms of Jesus? How might you intersect with the good news in such a way that you share that with others?

Dear God.
Please shine my weary soul with your love.
Fit me to bring the good news.
And, would you bless my feet en route, so I can bless others?
Amen.

DAY FIVE: TRAINING FOR THE HIGH SEAS

THE SHIPPING LANE TO GLORY

"WE ALSO GLORY IN OUR SUFFERINGS, BECAUSE WE KNOW
THAT SUFFERING PRODUCES PERSEVERANCE; PERSEVERANCE,
CHARACTER; AND CHARACTER, HOPE."

ROMANS 5:3-4

The winds shoved against us as the ferry rode the current of the Columbia River. This brief section of the river seemed quaint and tame, but the Columbia didn't get to be the fourth largest river in the U.S. because of its gentle qualities.[1]

Originating in Canada, the Columbia River winds through Washington until forming a boundary between Washington and Oregon. The mighty river makes a steady 1243-mile run for the Pacific Ocean. I wanted to belt out Woody Guthrie's "Roll On Columbia" while I snapped pictures and the wind blew mist into my face. Indeed, the power of the river could shift dark to daylight.[2]

Roll on, it does, generally in calm fashion. Until it reaches Astoria, Oregon, the Pacific Ocean entryway. Waves as high as forty feet chop away all thoughts of tranquility and friendliness.

There, the Columbia becomes a deadly force, one of the most dangerous bar crossings on the planet. Sailors and the Coast Guard dubbed this port "The Graveyard of the Pacific," because of the turbulence of this salt-and-fresh water meet-and-greet. So many ships have capsized that the Coast Guard trains its recruits there. If they can hold onto their ship in those high waves, if they can perform rescues in those stormy waters, then they can likely rescue anyone from about anywhere.

A display inside the maritime museum shows a boat clinging to the waves. Rather than horizontal on the water, the boat tilts at a terrifying 40-degree angle.

Once through that graveyard passageway, boats hit the wide-open Pacific Ocean, prepared for tumult or flat calm. The stormy passing bursts into endless vistas, horizons of brilliant sunset and spectacular dawns. The graveyard shift prepares them for the glory beyond the shoreline.

It's a little too close to home and real life, isn't it? Personally, I'll take the flat calm rather than the high waves. But we don't get to choose the weather. Staying on land isn't one of the options. Plus, imagine what we would miss. To get to the glory, we have to go through the turbulence.

So many struggle with serious seasickness on board this ship called life. Health issues. Unemployment or underemployment. Massive debt load, broken relationships, lost loved ones. Painful family situations. Disappointment darkens so many horizons, disillusionment creates whitecaps of the soul. It's so hard to hold on as the waves chop and churn. Far too many of us live a tad too close to emotional or spiritual shipwreck, and the decks are slick and we forgot our deck shoes.

I'm trying to remember that this passageway of turbulence is just this: a passageway. The meshing of our lives with God's best inevitably creates high waves, but the word *passage* is key. It's a shipping lane, a route out to the ocean vistas.

Paul's words to the people in Rome challenge me to stand on tiptoe, to peer over the waves toward the open seas. They invite me to learn to navigate the rough waters with a continual eye on the future. Not just heaven—though, what a pull that is!—but rather, our own emergence into real sailors and maybe, also, the Coast Guard. Perhaps these tough seas are our training waves, where we learn to hold on to the truth of God's faithfulness. We learn to grip the anchor of perseverance. We learn the skills necessary to help others in their "Graveyard of the Pacific" passages.

"I consider that our present sufferings are not worth comparing with the glory that will be revealed in us," Paul writes in Romans 8:18. *In us.* The glory to be revealed in us, shaping us for high seas sailing. Glory in us, and then through us. Not just one day in the far distant shores of heaven. Sooner, rather than later.

Grab a rope, mate, and hold on. We will get through this turbulence to the glory beyond.

Just Wondering...

Personally, I prefer flat calm with a cup of really good coffee. Describe one of those "flat calm" moments.

Training for the high seas sounds great—for someone else.

What sorts of training have you gone through, whether character, soul, or relationship? What fruits do you see from that training in turbulence?

How can you help others through their own rough seas?

Dear God!
I guess I need to be thankful for the turbulent waters,
if it helps me bring others to safety.
So, thank you. Reveal your glory in and through me.
In Jesus' name.
Amen.

WEEKEND TWO SEGUE

In what ways do you play it safe? In the current season of your life, how easy is it to turn toward God's wisdom, versus that of human beings? Consider the following words by Frederick Buechner, a theologian, pastor, and author.

Inspection stickers used to have printed on the back, "Drive carefully: the life you save may be your own." That is the wisdom of men in a nutshell.

What God says, on the other hand, is, "The life you save is the life you lose." In other words, the life you clutch, hoard, guard, and play safe with is in the end a life worth little to anybody, including yourself; and only a life given away for love's sake is a life worth living. To bring this point home, God shows us a man who gave his life away to the extent of dying a national disgrace without a penny in the bank or a friend to his name. In terms of men's wisdom, he was a perfect fool, and anybody who thinks he can follow him without making something like the same kind of fool of himself is laboring not under a cross but a delusion.

Frederick Buechner, Beyond Words[1]

This week's passages of scriptures follow.

> "As the heavens are higher than the earth,
> So are My ways higher than your ways
> And My thoughts than your thoughts."
> Isaiah 55:9

> "When Jesus landed and saw a large crowd,
> he had compassion on them and healed their sick."
> Matthew 14:14

> "And when you have turned, strengthen" the others.
> Luke 22:32

> "Stand firm then...with your feet fitted with the readiness
> that comes from the gospel of peace."
> Ephesians 6:14-15

> "We also glory in our sufferings, because we know that suffering produces perseverance; perseverance, character; and character, hope."
> Romans 5:3-4

READ OVER THE LIST SLOWLY, and invite the Holy Spirit to speak to you through one in particular.

Now, read that one tiny verse slowly. Then, wait. Let the words sink into your soul. Is there something God is highlighting for you? A word, or phrase, or challenge?

Next, ask, "What? What would you have me to do, God?" And listen for the answer.

REPEAT this process several times with the verse. Consider writing the "What" answer on a 3x5 card, and carrying it with you to apply throughout the day.

WEEK THREE

DAY ONE: STEP OUT OF THE TRAFFIC

A LONG, LOVING LOOK

> "BE STILL, AND KNOW THAT I AM GOD."
> PSALM 46:10

Most of the darting cars resembled caskets on wheels. People drove on the wrong side of the streets. They pulled across two lanes and stopped horizontally, waiting for an opening. Cars didn't brake and wave them in, but instead veered into the oncoming lane to continue their breakneck drive.[1]

Motorcycles slid in and out of traffic like a needle slip-stitching in fabric. Four lanes expanded beyond painted lines into eight. On the margins of every street, lean men pedaled oversized tricycles, their buggy seat crammed with as many as five passengers, including lolling babies clutched in the arms of small children.

I saw two stop signs. We stopped at neither. We careened along, made U-turns, parked backwards. Colorful cars like oversized birds honked tiny horns, variations on the Road Runner's *bee-beep*. The air, filled with the many-toned horns, did not seem to be filled with angry fists or road rage.

Pedestrian in the Philippines take their lives in their hands. To attempt to cross the streets borders on self-homicide. A vehicle was the only safe place. When I buckled my seat belt automatically, they teased me, "You must be from America." I looked at the traffic with its two seasons, crazy and insane, and laughed. "At least there we have rules."

With the cacophony of Filipino traffic in my ears, and the congestion and color filling my memory bank, Psalm 46:10 in the Message speaks deeply: "Step out of the traffic!"

The psalmist doesn't say, "Drive out," or "Pull over and park, get out of your car, sit on the curb and watch." He says, "Step out of the traffic." The implications are so personal, so immediate. To stand in normal traffic is life-threatening. To stand in the Bacolod City traffic and look anywhere but at the tin bumper cars around us would be suicidal.

Stepping out scares us; what would we do with ourselves? The psalmist says, "Take a long loving look at me, your high God."

Today, I took God's injunction seriously. I sat, not on the curb, but on a chair watching the world wake up. I corralled my brain traffic, silenced the honking thoughts, and focused. Just on God. Aloud, I began stating God's attributes, skirting around the schedule before me, zipping past the roadblocks of anxiety or fear or my toxic itinerary. "God, you know everything. You are loving. You are everywhere! You are present. All powerful. Mighty. Everlasting. Faithful. Your love never ends. Nothing can take me from your hands. You are the beginning and the end, the Alpha and the Omega."

I took a long loving look at this God, my Savior. My heart

started to sputter with gratitude. The noise receded. A smile replaced my rush-hour anxiety. I kept on. "You are merciful. You forgive me. You forget my sins. You are just. You are holy. You are funny." (Perhaps that's not one of the most common attributes for God, but we've had some good laughs together over zany antics and heavenly puzzle-building skills.)

Even now, remembering, I hear traffic in the background —we live on a major artery, just to drive the point home—and the downshifting of semis. I smile, and feel a little tremulous, as if I caught my beloved looking at me with eyes full of love.

Good thing I stepped *out* of the traffic. I would have gotten run over from distraction, with eyes like that.

Just Wondering...

WHEN DO you most feel the craziness of life?

HOW DOES it affect your relationship with God? With others?

WHAT WOULD "STEPPING out of the traffic" look like, for you?

Dear God,
Thanks for looking at me with such love,
and for calling me to life-saving practices. Help me to hear your love
in the silence, and change me with that love.
Amen.

DAY TWO: THE ENDLESS SONG

BEST. RULE. EVER.

> "I WILL BE GLAD AND REJOICE IN YOU;
> I WILL SING THE PRAISES OF YOUR NAME, O MOST HIGH."
> PSALM 9:2

Songs. We sing them, sometimes as inane merry-go-rounds in our head, like "The Song that Never Ends" that really doesn't. Or we lip-sync the meaning, moving our lips but not our hearts, as in, "Have Thine Own Way" and then refusing to forgive our neighbor, or our pastor, or our spouse or parents. Or we argue about their structure and form: "Guitar!" "No! Organ!" "Praise choruses!" "Hymns!" We split our worship services, or we split our churches. Sometimes both.[1]

Songs are powerful. Sing, praise, and worship are all commandments in the Old Testament, so songs are central to

God. Throughout scripture, the angels sing, churches sing, individuals sing. What power lies behind the command and the carrying out?

Don Campbell's book *The Mozart Effect* reports a variety of studies on Mozart's works, with effects that demonstrate radical changes in health, heart, and creativity. For instance, cows milked to Mozart's masterpieces produce more milk! Something to consider for dairy farmers. Mozart's music presumably reduces gang activity, raises SAT scores, shortens hospital stays for certain patients, lowers the need for tranquilizers, and raises the quality of rice for Saki. Good to know if you have a wet basement or need a new hobby.

Don't you love it when researchers uncover something profound that God revealed ages and eons ago? God had good reasons for commanding us to sing.

Moses' victory song in Exodus 15:1-18 celebrated God's deliverance of the Israelites from the cruel and bitter bondage of Egypt. Moses closed with praise and worship after reciting how God showed up to fight for their freedom. The lyrics clearly called the Hebrew nation to a right focus: remember who God is, remember how God cared for them, remember God's mighty works on their behalf. Singing this first song in their recorded history of faith surely brought the vagabond nation new hope and new trust, and invoked again their initial reaction after the Lord's remarkable deliverance:

"And when the Israelites saw the mighty hand of the Lord displayed against the Egyptians, the people feared the LORD and put their trust in him and in Moses his servant" (Exodus 14:31). Singing shifted their fear to faith. Singing pointed their hearts to God. Singing changed the singers.

Though I had responded to God's call on my heart as an adolescent through the hymn "Just As I Am," the first time I experienced a change in me and in my relationships because of singing was as a young, harried wife and mother. After isolating myself from my husband because of hurt feelings, after walling off my heart from reconciliation, I fumed alone in our empty parsonage. Rich had whisked the babies out for a long walk in the country to deliver them all from my dark presence.

In that empty darkness, that place of sin, God called to me, and challenged me, through pressure on my soul, to begin to trust and to sing. Quavering through a few choruses, I finally broke into tears. God began to heal me. When Rich returned home to a smiling partner, he asked, "What happened?"

No wonder songs split churches. Anything that directs us to God and to worship, the primary means of adoring the Trinity; anything that transforms us, the singer; anything so essential to communicating with God, others, and a broken world, the enemy wants to destroy, pervert, and damage.

Songs in worship are not about us, or about our likes and dislikes. Songs are about God, for God. Songs are about relationship. Songs call us back to our reason for being. They call us back to God.

And the One whose angels sing "Glory!" just waits for us to sing the words back. With eternity in mind, it really is a song that never ends.

Just Wondering...

How have you experienced God's presence in song? Is that a go-to means of prayer for you, or a churchy experience?

When has singing—whether your own or someone else's—caused a change in focus, attitude, presence for you?

. . .

I<small>F MUSIC IS NOT</small> one of your means of accessing God's presence, what about reading and meditating on the words to a hymn?

> *Dear God,*
> *This day I lift my soul to you in song.*
> *I rejoice in who you are,*
> *and praise you for your great and surprising love and presence in my life.*
> *Change me as result of singing to you.*
> *Amen.*

DAY THREE: RESCUED FROM A RED-LIGHT PAST

GETTING OVER SELLING OUT

"With you there is forgiveness, so that we can, with
reverence, serve you."
Psalm 130:4

People have pounded on her for years. Pastors preach against her wiliness and sinfulness, pounding pulpits about her self-centeredness.[1]

Yet, her story is my story. It is yours as well. It is Israel's story. It is the story of all believers. This red-light woman recently topped out my list of favorite people in the scriptures. Yes, Rahab. *That* Rahab. The presumed prostitute. The woman who pundits say used her body and who sold out her own people from her room in the outer wall of Jericho.[2]

The pounders expound that when the spies knocked on the door, she wanted to welcome them in a sexual way. Maybe we figure that between her prostitution and her lying—and who knows what else—there's enough evidence to justify some Rahab-bashing whenever her name comes up. Accusers accuse her of selfishness for guaranteeing her family's safety by helping the Israelite spies escape—for lying to save her own hide.

Not that we would blame her, particularly. The lie seems a small thing in the big picture of safety, of salvation for her family when soldiers returned to torch the city. Besides, what did she have to lose? Her lie is the least of her sins, if God were to measure sin.

I identify with Rahab – not because I have the same literal sin in my past, but because I have sin in my past, and likely my future as well. Period. My sin separates me from God, as did hers. All of our sins—big sins, little sins—cause us to "play the harlot," as scripture sometimes phrases it.

Rahab seems a rare human being. If, indeed, she were a prostitute, she chose to leave her "profession" and confess the God of Israel as her Savior. She opened the door on her shame and eagerly accepted the spies' offer of salvation. She agreed to live humbly outside the camp of the Israelites after being rescued, until at some point God brought her into community and she married Salmon. Scripture tells us he was the father of Boaz, whose mother was Rahab, Boaz the father of Obed, whose mother was Ruth, Obed the father of Jesse, and Jesse the father of King David (Matthew 1:5). Remember King David, the ancestor of Joseph, Jesus' adopted father?

According to Old Testament law, Rahab deserved stoning. But she broke with her past when she hung a scarlet cord in her window to signal Israel's soldiers. She chose a new side. Her hospitality to the spies and her confession of God's rule granted a new start and a place in the lineage of the King of the universe.

Who of us isn't Rahab? We have all sold ourselves for the

next paycheck, we commit spiritual adultery and stay away from our families. For acceptance we sell out our true identity and become a trophy spouse or friend. For the sake of peace we forfeit our gifts and play the "don't make waves" game. We tell jokes so people like us when our hearts are breaking.

We do this because of our wounds, because of our legitimate longings to be loved and accepted. So, too, was Rahab wounded. Ninety-five percent of prostitutes were sexually abused when young. They turn to prostitution out of shame or desperation, or in order to feel validated and loved: "If you touch me, I must be alive." Rahab deserves not our condemnation, but our sorrow about a society that abuses women and debases their humanity, and then judges them for sin.

What's your past? What wounds do you carry? Where have you felt the bruising of stones, judgment cast, love withheld? How have you sold yourself for love, for attention?

In our deepest wounds,
>   We want someone to remember.
>   Regardless of how hard we try to forget,
>   We want someone to see,
>   To care, to love us.
>   Regardless of all the ways we try to forget
>   God will not forget us. God sees our pain
>   God remembers our past
>   God longs to tie a scarlet cord
>   In the window of our walled city
>   And rescue us.

Just Wondering...

. . .

What sort of red-light past might keep sneaking up on you? Who pounds on you about it?

Sometimes we have favorite red-light issues to notice in others. (I usually find that somehow I am projecting my own secret sins and reacting to them instead of dealing with my own, honestly.) What are yours, and what do they reveal about you?

When have you experienced God's rescuing you? How?

Dear God,
Find me here in these wounds.
Help me to recognize others' wounds, and find them.
Amen.

DAY FOUR: KLIEG LIGHTS

THE BRILLIANCE OF VULNERABILITY

"Therefore confess your sins to each other
and pray for each other so that you may be healed."
James 5:16

Crockpot in arms, I flew into the church ninety minutes early, wearing hand-me-down workout gear. My sunglasses stayed in place, even after entering the building, because I wasn't yet wearing my face. The chili cookoff for the community lunch after the service needed our Symphonic Chili in advance—don't ask about the name; think, campfire songs and musical fruit—so I planned to drop and run, returning later dressed for church.[1]

Of course, while trying to slip in unnoticed and race out again like the invisible woman, or at least incognito, I met our pastor's wife at the door. She glowed in her white boat-necked sweater and her full church apparel.

What could I do but grin? And keep my dark glasses on. "This is a come-as-you-are party, right?" I asked.

She laughed sincerely. "I wish it were. Why don't you start the tradition?"

It's a thought. What if we decide to "come as we are" to church, in all of our un-finery? Just show up without the façade that masks our pain or anger or bitterness? What if church was a place where a key characteristic really was vulnerability, and openness about the true state of our souls?

Years ago, John Wesley gathered a small band of believers that met weekly for the purposes of truth and grace and growth. Wesley called these groups various names, one of which was Holy Clubs. Not "club" in the sense that we have exclusive membership, as in a country club, but in the sense of commitment to full participation. With vulnerability a primary requirement, the group members were expected to ask themselves daily and each other weekly these questions:

1. Does any sin, inward or outward, have dominion over you?
2. Do you desire to be told of your faults? Do you desire to be told of all your faults—and that plain and clear?
3. Consider! Do you desire that we should tell you whatsoever we think, whatsoever we fear, whatsoever we hear concerning you?
4. Do you desire that in doing this we should come as close as possible, that we should cut to the quick, and search your heart to the bottom?
5. Is it your desire and design to be on this and all other occasions entirely open, so as to speak

everything that is in your heart, without exception, without disguise, and without reserve?

Ouch! It's one thing to answer yes or no to those questions, yes being the preference. That would get us in the door. But how would it be to actually have someone ask, "What sin has dominion over you?" And then have another tell me of my faults? About as fun as tetanus vaccines, and I'd be about that open and eager to put myself under the examination. But if the requirement is vulnerability, a sinner always coming in an attitude of confession, contrition, and repentance? That would rock the world on its axis.

Imagine being open to another's listings of your faults. Imagine being in a group where people hear you confess your darkest secret, your ugliest sin, your most horrific temptations...and they love you, forgive you, and pray for you. Imagine people who cannot possibly sit in judgment of all the garbage hidden in your soul's basement, because they found a reeking dumpster in their own heart.

All the darkness would evaporate as forgiveness dawned with freedom, and then what glory would rest upon the faces of the people of God. It would shine into the world, like klieg lights over the fairgrounds.

By the way—better bring your sunglasses.

Just Wondering...

In what ways do you long for "come as you are" in church and in relationships? When have you experienced acceptance to that degree?

. . .

How does acceptance conflict with ideas of accountability?

This level of accountability and openness sounds, uhm, terrifying. To open ourselves up to others with such vulnerability? Yikes. But what if...? Consider your circle of friends, or of people you look up to as role models or mentors. What might change in you, to be surrounded by people safe enough to help you grow? What can you do, toward that possibility?

Dear God,
Help me to take off my sunglasses,
and not be afraid for you to see the sin crouching at the bottom of my
soul.
Thank you for accepting me, forgiving me,
and for helping me see others as you do.
Amen.

DAY FIVE: SAVING LIVES

AREN'T WE ALL MEDICS?

> "He brought me out into a spacious place;
> he rescued me because he delighted in me."
> Psalm 18:19

Smoke. Gunfire. Flames and screaming. Then the silent agony of death. Of dying and fear. He knelt, in the stinking dark on the ridge, his platoon either evacuated or left for dead. Casualties of war. "What am I supposed to do?" he begged God. "What am I supposed to do?"[1]

No answer.

Then, a cry from among the bodies and blood, the rocks and rubble. "Medic! Medic!"

He found his purpose, then, rescuing the wounded in the nightfall after the disastrous battle on Hacksaw Ridge. One by one, he dragged his comrades to the edge, harnessed them, and lowered them down the 400-foot sheer rock face until his hands bloodied. Exhausted, he surveyed the wreckage. "One more, Lord. Just one more."

Then one more, and one more. By the night's end, Corporal Desmond Doss saved as many as 100 soldiers.

All deemed, until his rescue, as casualties of war. Even the term undermines the reality. Casual? Rather than meaning, "no big deal, oh well," the root word originally meant, "fall." The fallen of war.

Corporal Doss searched for life where others saw death, and redefined triage: pulse equals life equals saving. Finding a pulse, looking the wounded in the eye, he found life. Where others saw death, he heard the panic plea for rescue, the depth of humanity: "Help me! I have children at home!" He stopped at nothing to save those lives.

As I greet people on the street, or in church, or at the grocery, I wonder about the battles people have fought, and are fighting. The strident woman I pass en route to my office. The student experimenting with substances. The adult caught in an affair, or embezzling. People suited up for success, or perching on church seats in decorum, but deeply wounded internally.

All around us, casualties walk, hobble, cripple; they blend in invisibly on their own battlefields. Or maybe we're so used to stepping around them that we turn blind to their presence, or to their wounds. We see photos on the news, watch videos on our phones in one-inch squares, trauma and devastation reduced to a virtual reality. But they are real, flesh and blood and a backstory of pain, of loss, of damage.

Casualties of war. And casualties of life.

Jesus knew the true reality: Each person, regardless of color or creed, bears scars from battle. Jesus' life and his stories, whether the good Samaritan or a dead child or the hunched-over woman or the hungry or sick or imprisoned, speak of help.

In the words of Corporal Doss, "With the world so set on tearing itself apart, it don't seem like such a bad thing to me to want to put a little bit of it back together."

The battle is not over. And we, you and I, are both casualties and medics on the battlefield. Hand over hand, prayer over prayer. "One more, Lord. Just one more."

Because life is worth saving.

Just Wondering...

When are you one of the casualties? How have others helped rescue you?

How can you keep others' reality in mind on a daily life basis: that they all bear scars, and have been in battles we cannot imagine? What difference will it make to be aware of that?

How might you be part of the medic team, that helps put the world back together, even in small ways?

Dear Great Physician,
You have saved my life, kept me from being one of the fallen.
Please allow me to recognize others' battles, and bring life.
Amen.

WEEKEND THREE SEGUE

Augustine of Hippo said, beautifully, "In my deepest wound, I saw your glory, and it dazzled me." I might experience God's glory in my deepest wounding. But often, I either hide from the wounds, or run to shame rather than God's glory. It's not one of my finer attributes.

However, it's not too late for light that leads to glory. This is a good week to invite God's light into the darkness in our souls, into our wounds, and into the world. It's such a logical progression: we find light in the love of Jesus, we begin to heal, praise results, we are able to be more vulnerable with others, and *voila*, more light results.

Then we become ready to be the medics, listening for those cries, watching the eyes of people we love, people we meet on the street. Medics, after all, are very aware of their own weaknesses. But they are also certain that in others' wounds, they can see God's glory. Hand over hand. Just. One. More.

THE SCRIPTURES TO review and meditate on this week:

"Be still, and know that I am God."
Psalm 46:10

"I will be glad and rejoice in you;
I will sing the praises of your name, O Most High."
Psalm 9:2

"With you there is forgiveness, so that we can, with
reverence, serve you."
Psalm 130:4

"Therefore confess your sins to each other and pray for each
other so that you may be healed."
James 5:16

"He brought me out into a spacious place; he rescued he
because he delighted in me."
Psalm 18:19

READ OVER THE LIST SLOWLY, and invite the Holy Spirit to speak to you through one in particular.

Read that one verse slowly. Then, wait. Let the words sink into your soul. Is God highlighting a word, phrase, or challenge? Next, ask, "What? What would you have me to do, God?" Listen for the answer.

REPEAT THIS PROCESS A FEW TIMES. Perhaps write the "What" answer on a 3x5, and carry it for all-day application.

WEEK FOUR

DAY ONE: OFFSTAGE VIEW

GOD IS WORKING BEHIND THE SCENES

"Therefore encourage one another and build each
other up, just as in fact you are doing."
I Thessalonians 5:11

In the award-winning movie, "Cinema Paradiso," the round little face peeked out between the thick velvet curtains. The child's dirty cheeks brightened with delight at the sight before him. His eyes sparkled, his mouth stretched into a brilliant half-moon of impish joy. He wasn't meant to be in the theatre, but once there, he determined not to miss a second of the show.[1]

Today, I feel like that child with a chubby-cheeked smile, sneaking a peek at a performance normally veiled to human eyes. What I see reminds me that, though the world outside the theatre be fraught with bad news, horror, sadness, and tragedy, beyond the realm of the visible, far more action occurs than I can imagine.

It's been one of those weeks. Or months, perhaps. A loved one wound up in the reality show called "The Belly of the Whale," as a friend titled it. That's agonizing for everyone, including those on the sidelines, far offstage, removed from the action and interaction. I don't know what's happening in the theatre of this one's heart, can't read between the lines, can't hear the cues called out from stage right or gauge audience response or even the actor's responsiveness to the cues.

The psalmist wailed in Psalm 88:18, "You have taken from me friend and neighbor—darkness is my closest friend." It feels as though the crew forgot the light cues, tech fell asleep on the job, the stage manager disappeared on a long coffee break.

Then, today, an email landed in my inbox.

"You won't remember me..." the sender began, "but we met when you spoke in my area..." nearly three years ago!

Then she said, "God has prompted me to pray for you, and I have been praying all week. Then God started insisting I let you *know* I'm praying—God can be so bossy!"

She had searched the Internet to find me, gone through my website. When she found me, I caught a tiny glimpse through the curtain. My soul responded with a huge sigh of relief, deep gratitude that God nudged her to pray then ordered her to let me know. What a miracle of perfect timing. Without divulging specific details, I told her about the belly of the whale.

She emailed back instantly. She would take this person to her prayer group. A group that meets every weekday at 5:30 to pray. As in, 5:30 in the morning. Saturdays, they sleep in. They wait until 7 a.m. to gather. "We've seen many answers to prayer since we started. Marriages, prodigal children, employment."

I wept at my keyboard, wept before God. God, who loves us enough to encourage someone a thousand miles away to pray. For *us*. This little obscure family in the Midwest. The curtain parted slightly, allowing a glimpse of a broader stage, an arena, a world full of events, prayers, miraculous workings that we cannot see with human eyes.

No matter what seems to happen on the reality show of a loved one's life—or my own life, or yours—the real picture is far bigger, guided by the usually unseen hand of the One who loves us more than life itself.

Just Wondering...

What's your belly of the whale? Or who do you love who's been in there?

When do you feel forgotten in those hard places?

How has God in the nick of time shown up for you, allowing a glimpse into your precious place in the great big world of God?

> *Dear God!*
> *Wow! Thanks for the peek into your great big work.*
> *Show me who I can encourage this very day,*
> *by prayer, a phone call, and your love.*
> *Amen.*

DAY TWO: IT'S IMPOSSIBLE

THE DANCE OF A KING

> "I AM THE LORD, THE GOD OF ALL BLESS;
> IS ANYTHING TOO DIFFICULT FOR ME?"
> JEREMIAH 32:27 NAS

Transfixed, I perched in front of the black-and-white television. Pumpkins, balls, fairy godmothers, and wicked stepmothers filled my world. In 1965, Lesley Ann Warren as Cinderella was the most beautiful person I had ever seen, and she deserved a prince's love. The ermine cape helped immensely too.[1]

But I was just a skinny kid, gawky, shy, and plain. Later that night, my heart hurt, and tears squeezed through shut eyes. I knew I would never be beautiful and never find a prince. Pulling the covers over my mouth, I cried myself to sleep.

Fast-forward to a recent spring, when instead of a vintage television set, I watched *Cinderella* from the front of a theater. Tall, lean, and gorgeous in black tails and snowy white shirt, my son waltzed before a ballroom backdrop, twirling his partner, smiling into her youthful face.

After curtain calls and congratulations, I left to lead a women's retreat. Like tireless dance partners, the lyrics would not leave my head. As insipid as the words may now seem to jaded, techno-bleary minds, Cinderella's music entered a world hungry for romance and a bit of intrigue. Protests and problems ravaged the sixties, but part of America still longed for the forever-after relationship of their dreams, Cinderella-style.

The simplicity of the musical's lyrics points to our timeless and deep-set longing to be loved: a woman pining for a prince, a prince longing for an angel.

Prince, princess, or pauper. Who wouldn't take the romance of a pumpkin turning into a carriage and mice into horses, clip-clopping the hopeful in magical finery to a ball where they find true love?

Many women at that weekend retreat lived with broken or breaking marriages, breaking hearts, and broken dreams. Their prince hasn't been real, only an imaginary invention of lovesick dreams, and they were heartsick. Some attendees were single—either they've never married, were widowed physically or emotionally, or were divorced or separated.

Whether male or female, so many of us bear scars from a daddy-prince who abandoned us, a father figure who abused and betrayed us, siblings who wounded us, mothers unable to properly mother us.

Content with pretend ballrooms, men and women spin about in the safe world of imagination. We disguise our disenchantment with would-be royalty—loved ones who end up fallible and full of foibles. We mask our disappointments with all sorts of behaviors, never realizing that there is a Lover who is crazy about us. Tragically, we sing another round of "It's Impossible!"

Glass slipper hopes aside, kings and princes didn't just sit around in golden thrones in golden palaces wearing golden crowns. They had countries to defend and battles to fight. Kings and princes were warriors, though in *Cinderella* their sole purpose is advancing the kingdom by throwing a royal ball to find a royal princess.

After finding her, Cinderella's prince remarks that he doesn't even know her name. But our Prince knows our name, our shoe size, and the number of hairs on our head. This Prince never leaves us. He thinks about us constantly. This Warrior fights for his people. This king dances with delight over his beloved, croons love songs, and shushes their fears with his love. This is the King about whom Zephaniah (see 3:17) writes:

> The Lord your God is with you,
>   is mighty to save,
>   And takes great delight in you,
>   God will quiet you with love,
>   God will rejoice over you with singing.

Cancel the casting call. Our Prince has already come. He has been searching for us forever, yearning to make our dreams come true and to satisfy our deepest longings. And impossible stuff is happening every single day...

Just Wondering...

WHETHER OR NOT YOU'RE hoping for a prince, you've

undoubtedly experienced the pain of broken relationships, disappointments in "wicked stepmothers", and the occasional (or frequent) anguish of loss or abandonment. Reflect on those for a few minutes. What have you learned about yourself there? About others? God?

When are you more vulnerable to the longing for that kind of love? And how do you tend to seek fulfillment of the longing?

Put into a few sentences your encounters with "impossible love." Who might need to know about that level of possible impossibility?

Dear Jesus,
You know my shoe size?
Show me today who needs to know your impossible love.
Help me to rejoice over others the way you rejoice over me.
Amen.

DAY THREE: WALKING THE LINE

WHOSE EXPECTATIONS MATTER?

"I WILL GIVE YOU EVERY PLACE WHERE YOU SET YOUR FOOT."
JOSHUA 1:3

"You can't walk no line!" June Carter threw the words at Johnny Cash at a rehearsal in Elvis Presley's hometown high school. Then she stalked out, leaving the tour.[1]

"I think John wrote that song for... everything and everyone he loved," the director of the 2005 bio pic *Walk the Line* said. "He was trying to walk the line for everybody, only everyone wanted different things, including himself."

How many lines have we tried to walk? Whether man or woman, employee or employer, parent or child? I have tried to lead right, dress right, smile right, act right, parent right, volunteer right, speak right, encourage right, write right, and pray right. I walked others' lines, trying to embody others' expectations.

This is not how the Christian life works. At least it's not the way God intended it to function, though we try to make it work this way.

But beneath the lyrics of my life, the promises to walk the line nearly destroyed me. Anger erupted over minuscule causes. Depression darkened the windows of my heart. Love for God disappeared and questions arose: "Is Christ real? Is Christianity impotent? Can Jesus really heal? Can he make all things new?" Like Johnny Cash, and the fracturing that followed, I finally realized that everyone wanted different things from me—different things, different works, different lines. Chameleon style, I shifted my appearance to blend in with others' expectations and demands.

In that broken place, I wanted to throw words and stalk out, June Carter style. But God held me close. The Comforter invited me to listen to my heart, to look beneath the lyrics for the truth. God invited me to watch whose line I walked. My performance needed to close. God asked me to drop the curtain on the past productions—to trust God to open a whole new show. In that loving and safe place next to God's heart, I quit the tour. I quit trying to walk everyone else's line, quit trying to please everyone and make everyone like me. Sometimes, I am more successful than others at leaving the tour.

Years earlier, God said to Joshua, "I will give you every place where you set your foot" (Joshua 1:3). This was no indiscriminate promise that Joshua could do his own thing or everyone else's thing and God would bless him. God's words were followed by the condition that Joshua walk the right line. God promised the Promised Land, a specific place, if the

Israelites would just trust their God and step out in faith into this territory.

After losing myself in our church's invisible job description, after losing myself trying to please every individual and committee at church, and after losing myself trying to endear myself to all my neighbors, I finally found myself.

There is a cost to this. When Jesus was healing, he headed the guest list—among the healed, at least. But the traditional church accused him of being from Satan. Jesus refused to walk anyone's line but God's, which placed him at the top of the Most Wanted list of the religious establishment. When you walk God's line, you may no longer be the MVP of the season or the top pick in the draft. Your song may not top the Billboard chart like Johnny Cash's songs did.

But the cost is worth it. When we lose ourselves to God, we find ourselves embraced in a love separate from performance, a love that blooms in God's promise: "I will never leave you or forsake you" (Joshua 1:5). God refuses to abandon us, and we learn anew the truth of being loved without expectation of performance.

What's next? Watch Christ open doors of ministry, using gifts you've never imagined. God changes the entire trajectory of our lives. Finally, then, we walk the right line.

Just Wondering...

LOSING OURSELVES IN OTHERS' expectations can be a simple yes at the wrong time. People will like our yes more than our no. No kidding. When have you said yes to the wrong thing, or for the wrong reasons? Why?

. . .

IN WHAT WAYS do you try to live up to others' "lines"? How have you lost yourself, or lost track of your own gifts and callings, because of that?

TRY INVITING the Comforter into the space of expectations, needs, and your yes and no. Wait there, then ask for direction. God loves to help us walk forward. Write here, what you hear and what you will do, or not do.

Dear God,
Please direct my feet onto the right path,
that I might follow after you and live into your gifts and calling on my life.
Amen.

DAY FOUR: YAKETY YAK

PLEASE TALK BACK

> "And pray in the Spirit on all occasions with all
> kinds of prayers and requests.
> With this in mind, be alert and always keep
> on praying for all the Lord's people."
> Ephesians 6:18

In 1958, The Coasters released "Yakety Yak." The song spent seven weeks at number one on the Rhythm & Blues chart. We learned the answering rule in childhood: don't talk back. We are not to talk back to our parents, teachers, pastor, or Sunday school leader. We are certainly not to talk back to God, nor to Jesus. Kids who talk back are sassy, ill-mannered, and poorly raised. We can hear a mother's words, "I taught you better than that."[1]

Wait, though. There's biblical precedent for talking

back to God—for a little repartee with Jesus. In fact, consider Jesus, walking the hills in Tyre, a predominantly Gentile area, trying to avoid contact with people. Still, the crowds race after him, following him everywhere. He cannot keep his presence a secret. A desperate mother—a non-Jewish mother—hears about Jesus and tracks him down (see Matthew 15:21-28). "Lord, Son of David, have mercy on me! My daughter is suffering terribly from demon-possession."

At Jesus' silence, the disciples leap into the chasm with their typical brusqueness toward intrusive people: "Send her away, for she keeps crying out after us." (Note: She is not crying out after the disciples. She cries out for Jesus. Interesting that the disciples interpret it in terms of their own inconvenience.)

Jesus answers her: "I was sent only to the lost sheep of Israel."

Jew or Gentile, to her it doesn't matter. Desperation drives her. How long has her daughter suffered? How long has the mother suffered trying to help her child? She flings herself at His feet. "Lord, help me!"

She will not be silenced by the disciples' rebuke nor by Jesus' silence nor his words. Love empowers her to stand in the gap, no matter the cost.

"It is not right to take the children's bread and toss it to the dogs." Jesus throws down this challenge statement, and seems to be waiting to see how far her faith will take her.

As far as is necessary. "Yes, Lord, but even the dogs eat the crumbs that fall from their master's table."

Imagine an enormous smile breaking out on Jesus' face. "Woman, you have great faith! Your request is granted." And that very hour, her daughter is healed.

Earlier this week, I sent out a prayer request for a loved one from the long-term list I rattle off before God daily.

Despite my constant beseeching, changes seem microscopic in this person's life.

A friend emailed me back, almost immediately. "Jane, don't stop praying. Pray and pray and pray. Don't give up." She told me her own story, begging God for her son's life, for his faith, for a future and hope. "I have thousands and thousands of hours of prayer invested in my son." He is now an upstanding man, husband, and father, loving and serving God with his whole heart. For a long time, though, he lived for himself and his own ends.

But God heard. God stored up the answer for just the right time.

So it is with us. Keep talking back to God. Keep telling God your hopes and dreams and longings for the people you love, for your own life, for your church, your community, your world. Keep rattling off your list. Rewrite it when it shreds from so much handling, when the ink runs because of your tears.

Don't let the crowd push you away from Jesus, running you off because you're bothering them. The truth is that faith —real faith—does bother people because it forces them to examine their own puny resources. Make noise before God. Someone's life may depend on it.

JUST WONDERING...

WHAT SORT of rules about back-talk did you grow up with? Or talking in general? (As in, "Don't talk with your mouth full." "Don't interrupt.")

HOW LIKELY WAS it that people in your family of origin were

interested in meeting your needs, if you did speak of them? When was that most likely, and least likely, to happen?

MAKE A LIST OF YOUR NEEDS, the needs and longings of others in your life. How much do you think Jesus wants to meet those needs? Take time and present the list to Christ, and wait there. Then start watching. Yakety yak. Life depends on it.

Dear God,
Thank you for welcoming my prayer requests,
and for being so happy to hear my voice.
This day, as I list my concerns, help me to trust you to do your will.
Amen.

DAY FIVE: ACTIVATING DYNAMITE

YOU'RE GOT THE POWER

"You have been clothed with power from on high."
Luke 24:49

Drive through the hills of southern Indiana, and every few miles you'll slip between a rock and a hard place. Literally, with limestone walls on both sides of your car. Archeologists and geological students often explore these stone faces, seeking rock-gems crammed with history, embedded with stories of the earth.[1]

But as a kid, my story isn't quite so deep. My granddaddy started his construction company with two pieces of equipment and parked them under a tree. They couldn't afford a garage, but gradually established a reputation and a business. The contract to build a section of four-lane divided highway near our hometown was a testimony to the company's hard and good work.

I pedaled my ten-speed bicycle on one of those roads before it was finished. Because of my granddaddy, I had special riding privileges as long as construction had quit for the day. The deep cuts, routed through the hills, showed long narrow tunnels in the limestone surfaces. Later I discovered they were drilled for dynamite to blast away the rock to make way for the road.

Our close connection to dynamite is more than just a family familiarity. Its inventor, Alfred Nobel, bequeathed his fortune to found the Nobel Prize, and deliberately chose the mighty word dynamite, from the Greek term *dunamis*[2] (δύναμις).

This explosive, rock-shattering substance is named after a word used to describe God's *dunamis*: great power, divine power, eternal power. I look at the quarries of my childhood, and the walls of limestone with their tubular impressions, in an all-new way. Those blasts are a picture of the power of God.

Guess what else the Greek word describes?

The power God gives us.

The power that raised Jesus from the dead, the power that "went out from him" in healing, the power of the Cross...*that* power, Jesus says, is ours as well. "Wait for it," he told the disciples, until you are clothed with dynamite-power from on high (see Luke 24:49). We wait for the power by praying, silence, reading scripture, gleaning wisdom, listening to God and one another deeply.

Power by itself, however, is dangerous. Nobel discovered that the explosive component of nitroglycerin had to be stabilized, and combined it with diatomaceous earth to make it transportable. In our dust-of-the-earth bodies, our humanity will forever be the reminder that the amazing mighty dynamic power of God we carry must be stabilized. Maybe that's why Paul coupled the dynamite-power with "love and self-discipline" (2 Tim. 1:7).

But even so, dynamite is impotent if not activated by fire.

Maybe action is the spark that ignites the power. By faith we know that the power that raised Jesus from the dead is ours to accomplish the work of Jesus in this world. Then we work it out.

Whatever rock-and-a-hard-place you're navigating, whatever stone wall you're encountering, whatever difficult conversation or relationship you're facing: pray, dig for wisdom, formulate a plan in line with God's purposes. Then light the fuse. Jesus sustains all things with his dynamite word (Heb. 1:3) and will sustain ours. Paul was strengthened by God's energy, which so powerfully worked in him (Col. 1:29). We act out that power to mighty good results, with God's mighty power. If we're clothed with power, then we're dressed for the day.

Let's get to work. We've got the power.

Just Wondering...

WHAT's your current "between a rock and a hard place" situation? Gauge your sense of powerlessness on a level of 1-10, ten being most powerful. What do you do when the number shrinks and your ability to impact a problem diminishes?

WHEN HAVE you experienced God's power in a place of weakness? How did you access or recognize God's power?

. . .

CONSIDER THE TRIAD: of power; the stabilizing influence of scripture, accountability, and prayer; and the activation. What are your primary stabilizing influences? How do you activate the power? What do you need to do, in a current hard place?

Dear God.
Help me to access your power.
Stabilize me with your word.
And do a mighty work through me, this day.
Amen.

WEEKEND FOUR SEGUE

Living a dynamic, *dunamis* life seems such a great idea. Theories usually do. But in the middle of the theory that a powerful life is possible, we have people and their needs and expectations. We have our own needs and expectations. We have circumstances. Plus, people.

Oh, I said that already. However, people may try to shush us, reminding us that others land much higher on Jesus' priority list than we do. (Maybe we are also the ones doing the shushing, because messy and needy people really do get in the way at times. Honestly.)

The strident voices of shame—that you will never be loved, never be enough, never measure up, always be a mess—hit all sorts of clanging discordant notes in our souls. Add in some unanswered prayer, a little "belly of the whale" time, and we have a recipe for defeated living. Whether it's our own life, or that of someone we meet, this is a real dynamic, and I don't mean dynamite. Although it could blow up.

Let's get off that defeat track for a minute and inhale. In. Out. As slow as you can possibly inhale, until your ribs expand and your stomach too. (No one is watching and no one actually cares about your belly right now.) Hold the air in your lungs, and remember God's word over you, "I've loved you with an everlasting love." (See Jeremiah 31:3.)

Now in a long, thin stream, exhale the air and with it the current shame occupying your insides. Wait with emptied lungs for as long as possible.

Inhale again, focusing on God's never-ending love, and hold that inside.

Exhale slowly another toxic topic polluting your soul, such as "It's all my fault."

Keep replacing the pollution with God's presence. Soon, your soul will be oxygenated with the truth, that you are deeply loved, truly forgiven, and absolutely called and equipped to make a difference in your world.

Because that's the absolute truth.

SCRIPTURES FOR THE WEEK, to review and meditate upon using Lectio Divina, journaling or another method:

> "Therefore encourage one another and build each other up, just as in fact you are doing."
> I Thessalonians 5:11

> "I am the Lord, the God of all flesh; is anything too difficult for me?"
> Jeremiah 32:27 NAS

> "I will give you every place where you set your foot."

Joshua 1:3

"And pray in the Spirit on all occasions
with all kinds of prayers and requests.
With this in mind, be alert and always
keep on praying for all the Lord's people."
Ephesians 6:19

"You have been clothed with power from on high."
Luke 24:49

WEEK FIVE

DAY ONE: I ONCE WAS BLIND

EMERGENCY FLARES

> "I'LL TAKE THE HAND OF THOSE WHO DON'T KNOW
> THE WAY,
> WHO CAN'T SEE WHERE THEY'RE GOING."
> ISAIAH 42:16, THE MESSAGE

His gifted hands caress the keys with a loving sightless familiarity, an intimacy born of lengthy relationship. He hears the music long-hidden in his soul through a keen auditory memory. Music pours from fluid fingers. A smile transforms his face. He lurches slightly forward and back in an indiscernible rhythm. The tawny dog rests on the floor beside the piano bench, a safe distance from the feet pumping the pedals of the grand piano.[1]

When the music stills, his hands move to his lap and he waits, head slightly turned toward the congregation. He does not wait for applause, though after a breathless rest, it attends his final note. Rather, a woman slips soft as a feather to his side, and he and his dog navigate the pews and aisles to a row closer to the door.

Afterward, when churchgoers mill about the lobby and the din of happiness rises, the woman by his side steers the well-matched couple of master and dog-guide through the throngs. In spite of his veiled eyes and the noisy confusion, the pianist seems content in the milieu.

But the decibels increase and crest at fortissimo, and the crowd crowds and suddenly, this tall, handsome man with his tight grip on his dog's lead, shoots his free hand in the air like a flagpole, or a human emergency flare. There is no panic on his face, as though he knows by faith born of experience what comes next. As I watch, separated by a crush of people, the feather-woman weaves to his side and guides him to safety.

So that, I think, is his signal for help. He stops, stands stock still, and raises his arm to heaven, trusting that someone will materialize and rescue him.

This morning, as I sat with my pen and journal, my tummy grumbling and my coffee cup empty, I stared into a dark yard and a dark world and worried dark worries. Most worries for most people seem to swirl about loved ones, and about clinging tightly on an untethered globe. My swirling worries were no different. I poured out my pleas while begging, "Please, please, please," but felt no relief from their noise and crowding.

Now, remembering, I raise my arm like the blind pianist, I who have physical vision but not the vision of faith, not today. I raise my arm, shoot my hand toward the ceiling and the heavens beyond, and wait. And listen. And wait.

Somewhere over my head the worries suspend, but do not abate. I lower my upstretched arm. Opening the scriptures to the week's Old Testament reading, the Isaiah selection I've skimmed for days transforms from mere words into crystallized hope at God's words:

> Take a good look at my servant...
> He won't brush aside the bruised and the hurt
> And he won't disregard the small and insignificant,
> But he'll steadily and firmly set things right
> He won't tire out and quit. He won't be stopped
> Until he's finished his work—to set things right on earth.
> Far-flung ocean islands
> Wait expectantly for his teaching...
> I'll take the hand of those who don't know the way,
> Who can't see where they're going.
> I'll be a personal guide to them,
> Directing them through unknown country.
> I'll be right there to show them which roads to take,
> Make sure they don't fall into the ditch."
> (Is. 42:1-4, 15-16, The Message)

INDEED. Someone has come to take us to safety. He won't be stopped until he's set things right on earth. Now I see.

As I watch, the worries blow away like feathers.

JUST WONDERING...

. . .

WHAT ARE YOUR SWIRLING WORRIES? Feel free to make a list. Getting them on the outside diminishes some of their power.

WHERE DO YOU FEEL BRUISED, hurt, or brushed aside? Lay that next to your worry list, and then align that with the words from Isaiah 42. What does Jesus, the servant spoken of in the passage, have to say about you, and about his plans and presence for you?

CONSIDER what sign you could make to remind yourself to seek help.

Dear Jesus,
Thank you! I raise my arm for help,
and trust that you'll guide me through this unknown country.
Thank you for coming to set things right.
In your name I pray,
Amen.

DAY TWO: LOOKING FOR ANSWERS

FINDING HOPE

> "Before they call I will answer;
> while they are still speaking I will hear."
> Isaiah 65:24

Delete. Delete. Delete. All the bargains show up in my inbox at zero-dark-thirty. I yawn over my coffee. I am at work too early to be conscious, let alone aware and ready to buy. Why am I on these lists? For 10 percent off at some place I will never shop? *Delete delete delete.* My cursor hovers over another notice. The header simply reads, Message. That seems redundant. But I know the sender and click.[1]

"Received a message to tell you a prayer has been answered."

Eleven words in the body of the email. I scratch my head.

Look out my office window. Adjust my one-dollar glasses. Scroll down on the screen for more.

Nope. That's it. Eleven words. No explanation.

I email back. "From God? For *me?*"

No response. I take that as a "Yes, of course, silly. For you."

God doesn't usually send me emails, and rarely downloads messages for me to share with others. Still, the God of the Impossible does seem to communicate clearly to others. I have zero doubt that God delivered a message through my friend.

But what prayer, exactly, has been answered? I've sent a boat-load of prayer requests to God's inbox. My email account shows 44,629 emails sent. Probably my prayer life is no different. I can get all beggy and needy with God.

Answers, on the other hand? I stare out the windows again. Decide on a walk in the young sunlight. I notice a surprise companion as I duck under branches, slung low over sidewalks: anticipation, as though searching for hidden presents. I'm on a treasure hunt. I realize I am smiling.

Didn't God say, Before you call, I will answer you (see Is. 65:24)? How about "Call to me and I will answer you..." (Jer. 33:3)? God told the prophets this thousands of years ago. Spoke through James, saying, "You do not have because you do not ask." The Psalmist reminds us, "God is faithful to all the promises" (see 145:13).

So why the surprise? Why haven't I lived in anticipation of seeing those answers? *[Insert mental shrug here.]* Haven't I been on the lookout, haven't I imagined God meant *me?*

While I walk, my soul turns to prayer, as usual when I can harness my mind. I try to thank God first, for love that never leaves, for grace that goes before us, for forgiveness in spite of my idiocy. And for this answer to a prayer, waiting to be revealed.

The list of requests is long—friends and family in varying stages of their dog-legged journeys of faith. My husband's calling as musician, composer, and pastor. My writing and speaking. Our calendars with their blank spaces waiting for God's filling. I shrug again, and open my hands. Not grabby, gimme-gimme style. Rather, a quiet opening, and also, a waiting and a watching to see God's answers.

Then the phone chimes. The first caller reports on a mentor for someone deeply in need, after years of my begging God. Check. Another: counseling for a friend after many years of imploring God. Check. By the day's end, five requests for ministry opportunities landed in my husband's inbox. Check check check check check.

This no-frills email yanks me back to the unnoticed reality of answered prayer. The smile on my face translates to my soul, and I shift to living in both anticipation and gratitude. In recognition and in hope.

P.S. If you send me your email address, I have a message for you...

Just Wondering...

THERE IT IS AGAIN. All the unanswered prayer business that clogs our faith-valves and blinds our eyes to God's loving presence in our lives. Speak aloud those requests, so your soul actually hears you asking.

TAKE A WALK, bearing in mind that there might be answers you haven't actually noticed. See if anticipation begins to lighten your step. Notice when you sense God's presence.

. . .

My friend's faith encouraged me and put a lilt in my soul. How might you encourage another who is weighed down with doubt?

Dear God!
Open my eyes to see your answers
to my miles-long list of requests.
You are faithful, and I watch with hope.
Amen.

DAY THREE: FROM FEAR TO FASTING

A LESSON IN GOD'S FAITHFULNESS

> "GREAT IS [GOD'S] LOVE TOWARD US,
> AND THE FAITHFULNESS OF THE LORD ENDURES FOREVER."
> PSALM 117:2

Skimming the previous year's journals, I spied an inescapable pattern. The ink, poured out over money worries, condemned me.[1]

Who knew, when we moved from a pastorate into a missionary-type ministry, that money would break my spiritual bank account? Every day fear gnawed: how would we eat, clothe our children, pay bills, cover the mortgage, even buy gas to get to speaking or worship events?

Sadly, it didn't only chew on me; contagious as the stomach flu, fear spread through our family. I snapped, nagged, interrupted, and otherwise tried to control my husband and three children. Buying milk only to see a sign elsewhere for two cents less panicked me. I drove the car on empty on the highway for miles, children nibbling their nails, because someone down the road surely sold gas more cheaply.

Check the math. If I saved even a nickel per gallon of gas, with a 16-gallon tank, we were talking about ninety cents. A tow truck, emergency interstate rescue, lives stranded, no husband or cell phone? That might have cost slightly more. Then again, fear is rarely rational.

In January, I decided not to worry incessantly about money. Checking my current journal, I counted only five references to money...in the first five entries.

I don't think that's progress.

Looking at this money anxiety meant examining my faith. What did I believe about God, if I obsessed over finances while following God's calling? Maybe God wasn't going to cover us. Maybe we used different calculators. Maybe our mortgage wasn't important to God, or the school fees that were due, or the electric bill. Maybe God wasn't a good God.

Maybe, in fact, God didn't really love us, and was playing a cruel game to shake us off the team. I cringed. The surgeon was isolating and probing a raw nerve.

Bookwork consumed this weekend. Three months since our last regular paycheck. A Mother Hubbard kitchen. Bills three inches high. So I followed my instincts. Chew, chew, chew.

At church, we embraced Psalm 117.

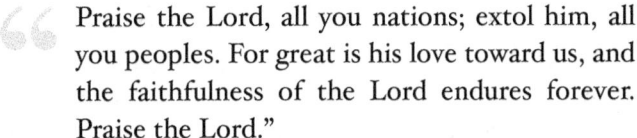
> Praise the Lord, all you nations; extol him, all you peoples. For great is his love toward us, and the faithfulness of the Lord endures forever. Praise the Lord."

The entire service pointed toward God's faithfulness, and our response: praise.

Faithfulness is God's character, God's love toward us so great that God can't *not* be faithful. My head went down. I reviewed the ledger mentally: numerous years of this ministry. Our clothes haven't worn out. Our cars are worn but (usually) running. We have little debt. None of us is losing weight from privation. We use the gifts of words, music, and speaking that God called us to use. Praise bubbled up and tears leaked out. The pressure on my chest lessened.

Still, worries descended again, even after my daily reading included Philippians 4:19: "My God will supply all your needs according to his riches in glory in Christ Jesus."

I decided to put this to the hunger test. Fasting for a day, every single time I felt hunger, I would pray. That God would meet people's needs through us and meet our needs through God's people. Or however God chose. That God would be God. (Just a note: God is always God. My faith does not increase God's God-ness, nor my lack of faith diminish that. However, I'm being honest about this journey, and that is part of my learning.)

This was about God's riches, not mine; about rejoicing in the Lord, whose love endures forever. And about my inability to be God anymore. (As though I was *ever* God.)

I haven't checked the mail today. I doubt there's a check underwriting this month's business and personal expenses. Maybe there is. But this is not about expenses versus income. This is about God. When I felt hunger just now, I rested my head on my desk. "Oh God. You have everything we need." My brain did a jolt. "You are everything we need. In you, we have everything."

Hunger reminds me that my deepest hunger is not relief from monetary pressures. My deepest hunger is to be well and truly loved (Proverbs 19:22). And only God can do that.

From fear to fasting to God's faithfulness. It is worth the journey.

Oh, and the mailbox? Two checks. Enough for groceries and gas. I think I'll make a celebration dinner. Because God's love endures forever. And for today.

Just Wondering...

For most of us, some sort of issue becomes our go-to. Maybe it's money, or safety, or relationship intimacy, or... What is yours? How or when does it show up?

How does it affect your relationship with others? With God?

How do you think God really feels about you and your well-being? What does Philippians 4:19 say to your soul and your go-to issue?

> *Dear God.*
> *You are everything we need.*
> *Help me to trust today.*
> *To trust, even for the next five minutes.*
> *And then, the next five.*
> *Amen.*

DAY FOUR: PACK RAT

BENEATH HOARDED THOUGHTS

> "Get rid of all bitterness, rage and anger,
> brawling and slander,
> along with every form of malice."
> Ephesians 4:31

A relative stacked and stashed and stored, collected and cached all manner of odds and ends, large and small hodgepodge. So much so, that by the end of her life only a narrow walkway through the rooms and hallways existed. The attic bulged until the joists below seemed in danger from the weight of the items in storage. Alleyways snaked through the only two rooms left accessible in the home.[1]

What a colossal assortment of junk, pure junk—nothing of value until reaching either the very bottom layers, or the margins of the room, where some antiques groaned beneath mountains of worthlessness.

Pack rats, the desert rats after which we nickname this disorder, collect for their nests an assortment of sticks, leaves, twigs, and shiny bright objects that grab their attention. Piece by piece, these rodents haul items to their nest and build it into a dam-like structure, sometimes as big as four feet across. They collect for reasonable reasons: a place to sleep, protection from their enemies, protection from severe heat and cold.

Human hoarders collect for reasonable reasons too. The need for safety and shelter; possessions help them feel secure. Memories of want, the pain of not having physical or emotional needs met, also opens the door to hoarding. Perhaps they haven't received enough love from others. Or they simply score low on the organizational-ability scale.

Though my husband might disagree, I am not an excessive hoarder of material goods. Still, I do have an inability to organize: closets, piles of mail, filing cabinets, refrigerators, my thoughts.

Recently, my stomach roiled to discover a hidden hoard. It surfaced when I went away for a mini personal retreat. I needed distance to sort through some piled-high alleyways in my brain, too many thoughts jumbled together to make any sense. I headed off to pray and journal and read scripture and be still.

In that stillness, a conversation came back from the previous night. My son and I were headed to church, where he would leave for a retreat. He seemed distant—unusual for our garrulous child. "What's wrong?" I asked, patting and rubbing his shoulder.

"I hate it when people are angry." Meaning, people like me. He'd overheard some emotional volleys I'd lobbed that evening.

"I'm not angry, honey. Not at you. Not at anyone."

But on Saturday, as those words flooded back, I cranked open the curtain to reveal a warehouse-sized collection of hoarded upsets. I was angry. At people who'd wounded me from the past or wounded someone I love. Angry at God. Angry about some problems that showed up en masse from all directions. Beneath my jumbled thoughts seethed a volcanic mountain.

According to one website, "Hoarding is the excessive collection and retention of things or animals until they interfere with day-to-day functions such as home, health, family, work, and social life. Severe hoarding causes safety and health hazards."[2] Well, obviously. Hoarding behavior has clear health and safety issues for collectors. Newspapers or clothing can ignite, and diseases from animals can spread. Socially, collectors' worlds shrink to include only their personal space, which shrinks ever further with each addition to the piles. Loneliness must pervade their days, even as they collect the stuff meant to allay that very isolation.

Hoarding drains energy through the resultant clutter and chaos. If a pack rat gets under the hood of your car or into your attic, it creates loud havoc with the engine, the wiring, or the insulation. That would explain the commotion in my thinking. My own rat-packing chewed the wires of my relationships. Intimacy in the midst of unacknowledged anger is tricky, if not impossible.

Time to inventory. How had I perceived these items as valuable? The list was ugly, the collection suitable only for the dumpster. No resale value, no summer garage sales for me. I made my list, as painful as it was, because I wanted to be free. How appalling to see how long the list and how old some of the incidents. "In repentance and rest is your salvation," says Isaiah 30:15.

There's nothing like a clean house. The problem is in

keeping it clean. Now I try to sort every day, take inventory every night, and get free. No more warehousing, no more fire hazards. And lots more room for relationships.

Just Wondering...

Where do you fall on the spectrum of order vs disorder? Love to clean, loathe to clean? Clean for company, clean regularly, clean never?

What sorts of stashes have you uncovered, whether through helping a friend or loved one, or cleaning out your own closets? How about soul-stuff? What kind of things do you hoard? Good memories or painful?

How do repentance and rest relate to one another? And how do they fit into any hoarding or stashing you have? What do you want to do about it?

> *Dear God,*
> *I wait with my list, and then offer it to you.*
> *Help me to stop hoarding sinful reactions,*
> *and start collecting your forgiveness, peace, and joy.*
> *Amen.*

DAY FIVE: CLOSE ENCOUNTERS OF THE HEALING KIND

WHEN GOOD NEWS TRAVELS

> "Those with diseases were pushing forward to touch him."
> Mark 3:10

Such a crowd. Like a county fair without the rides and cotton candy. Sticky, sweaty, pushy people. The rave reviews rippled throughout the country in waves of astonishment and an entirely foreign hope, and people were desperate to get closer. If only they could lay a finger on his clothes, make contact. Crutches and canes, oozing sores and paralyzed tongues... Come one, come all.[1]

They sure did. Straight to the miracle worker, the only man they'd ever heard about, who actually healed people. Except for way back in the years of the great-great-grandparents, so long ago, the stories about prophets like Elijah assumed mythical status.

Suddenly, right here in the flesh, the Miracle Man stood before them. People clamored and stretched, the words of their friends branded on their souls. "This man healed me."

Turns out, good news travels.

Before we turn away from this good—no, amazing *and* good—news, because we don't see radical healings happening today, consider this.

Mark 3:10 reads, "For he had healed many, so that those with diseases were pushing forward to touch him."

Pushing. *Pushing* forward to touch Jesus. What an image. People so aware of their own infirmities they fling themselves toward healing. It's not exactly one I see in my own private life, nor too often in the public life of the church. We aren't always even aware of our broken places, much less flinging ourselves toward Jesus for healing. Desperate? Not usually, at least, not once we're inside the hallowed walls.

Maybe we have a shortage of healing happening through our churches because we have never really experienced that level of healing ourselves. Theoretically, the altar could be jammed with all of us, every single Sunday, stretching out our grubby souls for help.

Maybe we're embarrassed or ashamed or in denial of our towering anger or the bitterness lining our soul. Heaven knows, I sure am. Further, who wants to confess to jealousy or razor tongue? Crutches, canes, oozing sores? We can't possibly go public with these messes. Confession and self-examination are *so* out of style.

But the people in Jesus' time, with their obvious physical issues and spiritual demons, their outcast state of being, felt no such shame. They had the sense to run to Jesus, to press forward to the One who could heal. The only One, in fact.

About that word, *heal*. In the original language, it's *thera-*

peuo'. Besides meaning to literally and physically heal, it means to serve. To give help. To take care of another. From this original root, we come up with therapy, therapeutic. All under the branding of serving, helping, caring.

Wait. It isn't fancy worship, or padded seats, or awesome overhead monitors that change the (church) world? It isn't high tech Sunday school or purpose-driven programming and a great vision statement? It isn't glitzy online services and sleek speaking? Not free coffee cups for every new face? (Although, honestly, really good coffee might help.) What did Jesus say, after so many of these close encounters of the healing kind?

"They will know you are mine if you have love..." (John 13:35). Love outside the walls and inside them, too.

Love. Wrapped in good old-fashioned acts of service, with the name of Jesus on them and the power of Jesus in them.

Therapeuo' as we work and drive and shop and mingle. Imagine waking up and moving through each day with the primary agenda of serving, giving help, taking care of others. All in the name and power of Jesus.

I'm betting on a stampede.

County fair, anyone?

Just Wondering...

WHAT KIND of reaction might you have, to hear about a "miracle man" who was doing crazy things like healing the lame and raising the dead? Do you think you'd feel differently about a first-century experience versus this year?

SOME OF THE ideas about personal healing include vulnerability to hearing where we need to grow, confessing our messes, asking for help. How have those helped you to heal, or how might they?

WHO DO you know who is desperate for healing? What would *therapeuo'* in its full sense of helping, serving, caring and healing look like?

Dear God,
You can do anything—including heal me.
May I pass along that healing
through helping, serving, and caring for others.
Amen.

WEEKEND FIVE SEGUE

While rehabbing their house, a friend built a tent in the backyard so everyone could escape the noise and dust. Seeing it, I exclaimed, "What a perfect place for a personal retreat!" We laughed, but seriously? Yes.

Maybe it's not a tent in the backyard. (Although, why not?) Maybe it's a 30-minute walk by yourself where your own soul is the only priority. Not phoning, texting, scrolling social media; not work, or relationships, or duties. Just you and your soul.

Perhaps one day a month would work, where you arrange for the world as you know it to continue to spin, and you leave for three, or six, or eight hours. Monasteries have beautiful grounds to walk and pray. There's a nationwide network of arboretums. State or local parks, coffee shops, camps and retreat centers work as getaways. Where could your soul breathe in and out, and refuel? Could you make a plan to get there?

One benefit is perspective. An artist paints up close, typically, but steps back from the canvas to see the big picture.

Oops, too dark there. That shadow isn't right. Need a pop of color here, or better detail. At a distance, the artist assesses what's working, what's not working, given the overall canvas view. The same for us: a personal retreat offers a big picture. Otherwise, we easily over-focus on tiny details or a particular quadrant, and forget what God's bigger picture might be for our life. We think we're mired in the clouds but wait, there's sunshine!

The logistics of a personal retreat, whether one hour or a day, require planning. If you have children, what about trading a day with a friend? Where can you go, and what might you do during your mini getaway? Some ideas: journal, draw, meditate on scripture, read a contemplative author you appreciate, listen to and/or sing a hymn or praise music. Walk, dance, run, paint, intersect with God creatively as your soul refills.

Ultimately, it's more godly to operate out of God's fullness than our emptiness. Here's to a full tank!

SCRIPTURES FOR THE WEEK, to review and meditate upon using Lectio Divina, journaling or another method:

> "I'll take the hand of those who don't know the way,
> Who can't see where they're going."
> Isaiah 42:16, The Message

> "Before they call I will answer; while they are still speaking I will hear."
> Isaiah 65:24

"Great is [God's] love toward us, and the faithfulness of the
Lord endures forever."
Psalm 117:2

"Get rid of all bitterness, rage and anger, brawling and
slander,
along with every form of malice."
Ephesians 4:31

"Those with diseases were pushing forward to touch him."
Mark 3:10

WEEK SIX

DAY ONE: THE BRIDGE

FIND A LITTLE CONNECTION

> "Greater love has no one than this:
> to lay down one's life for one's friends."
> John 15:13

With a wide smile, Melissa gestured at the scenery as she and her husband Kurt strolled across Westminster Bridge. Wrapped in coats and hats to guard against London's chill and fog, they'd arrived just a couple of hours earlier for a one-day sightseeing whirlwind. The European tour celebrated their Silver Anniversary.[1]

Starting toward the steps at the end of the bridge, Melissa heard a screeching. She turned and saw an oncoming car's hood bearing down on her. Her next memory is from the ground.

Her husband, "the love of my life," she said, shoved her from the car's trajectory. The vehicle struck Kurt, propelling him over the bridge headfirst to the pavement below.

By the time Big Ben struck 3 pm, Melissa was a widow. Her life would now be marked as Before and After. Before March 22, 2017, when she was a wife rejoicing in 25 years of marriage. And After. After Khalid Masood drove his car at 30-miles-per-hour into pedestrians on an 82-second killing spree.

She wiped away tears in an interview[2] over 18 months later. Kurt "pushed me out of the way of the path of the car. He basically sacrificed his life for mine." She gulped in air, grateful for his action. But, honestly, she said, whether or not he knew them, "He'd have done it for anyone. He was that kind of guy."

In an era of me-first or even me-only, Melissa's words freshly convict me. "He sacrificed his life for mine." So few people experience such a trade, another's life for our own, certainly not literally. In fact, figuratively speaking, so many people feel as though they've been thrown *under* the bus rather than *saved* from it. Further, haven't we all been betrayed? Wounded by people who should love us, or by people who haven't even met us and with no reason to hurt us? Haven't we also been the people who did the wounding?

Into this certainty—that we are both the wounded and the wounding—comes this rock bottom truth. We *have* experienced the trade-off, your life for mine, of which Melissa speaks, whether we acknowledge that or not. One Man traded his life for mine. For yours. It didn't matter if he knew us—though he knew us from eternity past—or watched us botch up our own lives and the lives of others. It didn't matter if we were complete strangers to a church, or to any sort of faith at all, or to a baby born in a manger who'd grow up and hang on a tree for the exchange.

In a love-defining, premeditated act, he traded his life. An action that both defines real love and invites us to join the demonstration. "This is how we know what love is: Jesus Christ laid down his life for us" (1 John 3:16a).

"Yeah, yeah, yeah," we say. Stifle a yawn. "Sing me a new chorus, okay? We know all that."

But I'm not sure it's come home in exactly the same way as for the woman who woke up a widow on Westminster Bridge.

Melissa Cochran grasps the reality of this exchange, her husband's life for her own, and offers a watery smile. "I was grateful to be alive. It's really hard without him...but knowing that he saved me sure makes me want to make him proud and recover as best I can."

He saved her, and she wants to make him proud as a result. My throat closes. I have acted in ways that probably don't make Jesus proud. Maybe that's true for many of us.

Melissa goes further. Does she hate her husband's murderer? "He didn't have the compassion for humans that Kurt did." Her eyes again fill with tears. "If we could all find a little connection with each other, maybe some of this hate would go away."

Compassion and connection make the hate go away. That bridge would make Jesus proud.

JUST WONDERING...

WHAT IS a Before-and-After moment for you, that changed your life? Or the life of someone you love? How did that impact you?

. . .

How do you define forgiveness? Where do you struggle to forgive another person? No shame in acknowledging that; it is a real-life issue. When we're hurt, forgiving the one who hurt us is a challenge. How does holding on to the hurt help? When have you forgiven someone for a monumental problem, and how did that go for you?

We've all acted in ways that wouldn't make Jesus proud of us. But that doesn't have to be our life story. How can you find compassion for your own losses, and where would you like to offer compassion for others? How will that help?

Dear Jesus.
Please give me your compassion for others,
and bridge the distance with your love.
Help me to help make the hate go away.
Amen.

DAY TWO: R.S.V.P AND A.S.A.P.

OPENING THE MAIL

> "BEHOLD, I BRING YOU GOOD NEWS OF GREAT JOY
> WHICH WILL BE FOR ALL THE PEOPLE."
> LUKE 2:10 NAS

Invitations crowd both the porch mail box and the spam file. Buy a walk-in bathtub. Get premium home or life security. Power-up your sex life or eradicate toenail fungus or lose 122 "lbs. of flubber" or meet your love match. Buy this suitcase, eat that super food, vote for someone or something. Book a flight or reduce your carbon footprint. Purchase a new car, or life insurance. Or an IRA. Or all three. Invest here, give there, start your exercise program *today*.[1]

We're invited every day to more possibilities than we could ever entertain or afford, and some we would never even imagine. A few invites are relevant, and some are, shall we say, poorly targeted.

And then there's the day the invitation arrived, straight from heaven, wrapped in rags, scented with hay and dusted with donkey dander. Perfectly targeted, easily missed, often overshadowed because of the packaging: A baby? To meet our deepest longings? A pregnant teen? A husband ready to divorce his wife? Not a very slick marketing campaign, seems to me.

Except for the core longing that invitation addressed then, and still addresses now.

That pile of invitations in the mail, those jamming your spam file, all seem to contain a similar theme: *this will make your life better. Respond immediately, offer ends soon.*

This manger invite, with no expiration date, promises to meet that longing on a core soul level. An ongoing summons to be deeply loved, to be changed by that love, to love forward.

Somehow, this invitation gets lost in the influx of wrapping paper, credit card bills, company, and holiday expectations. By December 25, I've easily lost track of the summons to live meaningfully, to R.S.V.P. Maybe we give it another stab on January One. But, you know, the best laid plans... So easily waylaid by bigger, better, brighter. And busy.

In this current season, I'm re-sorting my mail. This invite comes first, and I decide to respond to the crazies with my breath and with music.

When advertising and expectations bully me—buy this, decorate that, give yet another gift—I stop and breathe. One of the names for the Holy Spirit is *breath* in scripture. Exhale the stress, inhale the peace of God. Exhale fear. Inhale heavenly comfort. Big deep breaths tell our brain and body, "This is not a crisis; you do not need to fight or flee right now."

Comparison-itis attacks. I grab a hymnal, and sing (however off-key) a favorite Christmas carol. The music speaks to my soul and mind in ways that other verbal cues miss, adjusting my toxic fret-levels. I seek application from *Joy to the World*, "No more let sin, and sorrows grow." Where do I? How do I stop that business?

Is there a practice behind the lyrics, for instance, of *Silent Night*? How about applying that to a minute, or five, today? Just sixty seconds or so, when I am quiet, and my attention directed to heaven and to what God might speak into me. Maybe the mountain doesn't shake, the bush doesn't burn, oracles don't peal. But if I wait, and listen, quiet love wallpapers my soul.

A heavenly invitation. A holy longing. Heaven comes to earth.

This year, say yes.

Just Wondering...

How do you handle all the ads and mailers and "gotta-haves" so prevalent year-round? Where and when are you vulnerable to comparison-itis?

What's one of the most fun invitations you've ever received? Or offered? If you could be invited to the event of your choice, what would that event be?

What about this invitation from heaven? How do you respond, even now? When do you experience a holy longing? What is your relationship with Jesus? Friend? Good guy? Role model? Helper? Savior?

Dear God!
An invitation to me? *I say yes, and now invite you to quiet my soul. Show me where sin and sorrows grow. Please rid them out, that I might sing* Joy *again, to this weary world. Thank you for sending Jesus, our personal invitation to enter into heavenly peace right this very minute.*
Amen.

DAY THREE: THINKING CAP

GETTING IN OUR RIGHT MIND

> "THE PEACE OF GOD,
> WHICH TRANSCENDS ALL UNDERSTANDING,
> WILL GUARD YOUR HEARTS AND YOUR MINDS
> IN CHRIST JESUS."
> PHILIPPIANS 4:7

Closing the office, I grabbed the laptop to bring on the road. Then I set down the computer to first pack a water bottle and slug down my coffee. Put on my coat. Couldn't find my keys. Got to the door without the computer. Couldn't find it, but first needed its M.I.A. case. Five minutes later, I found the computer after locating the case, misplacing my phone, and switching into street shoes.[1]

Possibly, sleep would help. My fancy-schmancy hand-me-down watch tracks my sleep habits. They aren't anything to write home about. Fatigue leads to forgetfulness.

Plus, we have brain drain from screens, constantly flipping images. On my current flight, each seat-back sports a personal television monitor. Mine turns off. My neighbor's off-switch seems to be broken; I know this because I tried to turn it off while she was sleeping. Her screen changes scenes less than every six seconds, by my layperson calculations. "But who's counting?" asks the woman with A.D.D. (i.e., me).

Between information and images pelleting us, and lack of sleep, no wonder we struggle with mental fatigue. No bandwidth. Brain strain. Or drain. We live in the middle of "I can't think straight" times and discover, along the way, that it's become a way of life and a default excuse. "I forgot." "I wasn't thinking."

"Put on your thinking cap," my mother used to say. I never understood how one could appropriate such head wear. Hats aren't becoming on me, but at any given time I would have liked to buy such a cap. Or two, one to wash and one to wear.

Recently, someone reached out for help with mental exhaustion, asking only that I pray extra hard. I overheard my soul praying the scripture, "We have the mind of Christ" (I Cor. 2:16).

Really? How often do we think with that tool? What does that even mean? And how do we access that Brain scan? My mental record more accurately reflects the Old Testament. The prophet Isaiah records these words from God: "My thoughts are not your thoughts, neither are your ways my ways" (55:8).

My thoughts exactly.

If I have the mind of Christ, then I start to ask him, "What do you think here? What might you do, in my shoes?

What words would you offer this wounded person who just wounded another? How does love look and act, right now?"

Recently, in a sleep-deprived state, I pounded out a testy email. Without putting anyone's address in the TO slot. Ooh, I sounded off, really laid it on the line. Full disclosure: hitting send would have destroyed my reputation in that community. Thankfully, I waited. Returned to it later, deleted 99% of the contents, and came up with a sentence that wouldn't make Jesus look bad. Or me either, for that matter.

Sometimes, we ask, "Jesus. What do you think about me, right now?" Because my earth-brain sometimes receives a flashing error message. Warning: defect. Loser. We need to get the truth on our belovedness, friend.

We fix our minds on Christ, get Jesus' thoughts, seek out his words. And we listen, which according to my parents, meant obey.

Henri Nouwen suggested that Christ's words were born from silence, from listening deeply to God. Maybe, in our noise-lambasted world, we need to shut our mouths. To seek out silence and turn our minds and hearts toward the One who speaks in stillness.

And in loudness. And in nature. And through the scriptures. And through people. And...

Maybe that thinking cap is more than wash and wear. It's all day, all night access. Meanwhile, as we're accessing, we'll keep the TO space blank. Until Christ's thoughts become our thoughts. Then Jesus looks good on us, to a weary world.

JUST WONDERING...

HOW MUCH SLEEP do you get on average per night? Does that seem ideal? I function better brain-wise and memory-wise when I am more rested, though I can't always change that. Also, hydration helps. When do you have brain-drain or a teeny memory issue?

How about information overload? Headline headaches? What do you do about these wearisome conditions? What do you want to live with?

The tool of quiet interests me as a means of healing brain strain. What if you try that for thirty seconds? A minute? How else might you rest your brain and soul, and access Christ's presence? What will you do? Perhaps you can create a "Mind of Christ" prayer that is your go-to. For instance, "Help needed here."

Dear Jesus.
I need your thoughts, I need your mind working in me.
Please help me recognize my own brain bombardments and deficits,
and listen in to your heart now.
Amen.

DAY FOUR: THANKING YOU IN ADVANCE

SHORTHAND FOR FAITH

"Behold, I am doing a new thing;
now it springs forth, do you not perceive it?"
Is. 43:19 ESV

The bank's ceiling soared overhead, an arch of gilded art. Polished wood counters, metal grillwork, gleaming white marble.[1]

Not bad for my first real job. Except for the terror. This sixteen-year-old was entirely unqualified for banking. But once my fingers stopped shaking, my summer job in bookkeeping, filing checks in the back room, anchored me. Because I kept saying yes, they trained me as a floater, slipping in for the tellers at lunchtime and on their vacations.

Then, they wondered, could I fill in for the receptionist, who, P.S., was also the secretary to the president?

Since my heart tumbling about my chest did not result in an all-out heart attack, I said yes. I knew John Robert Gregg's Shorthand, after all. Kind of. I might or might not have filled in a lot of missing or unlearned squiggles with abbreviations and cramped cursive.

Turns out, nearly every letter the bank officials wrote ended with,

> Thanking you in advance, I am
> Very truly yours

Their signature followed. From my teenage viewpoint, the "complimentary close" resonated with power and prestige. Of course the bank directors deserved cooperation.

Now, it seems quite an assumption: that the recipient of the letter would comply with its author, whatever the subject matter entailed.

Though I worked at the bank on school breaks through college, I hadn't thought about this closing line for years. Then one day, while walking, I began thanking God for answers to prayer that were en route, but not yet visible to me. "Thank you for my friend's coming job. Thank you for the needs you're meeting. For the ways that you're providing. Thank you for healing so-and-so. Thank you for the work you're doing."

I wasn't praying in 1888 shorthand, or in 1976 bank president-ese. I was agreeing, instead, with words scribed (not in shorthand, but in Hebrew) by Isaiah, from far longer ago. "Behold, I am doing a new thing; now it springs forth, do you not perceive it? I will make a way in the wilderness and rivers in the desert" (Is. 43:19, ESV).

God didn't say, "Keep watching, because one day if you hold up and are still around I'm gonna do a new thing." No, God said, "I'm doin' it. Now. Don't you see it yet?"

I decided to work on my prayer penmanship. I don't know who learns shorthand or even cursive anymore. But I know this: part of every single day, I plan to sign my verbal prayer letters, "Thanking you in advance..." We can live into the truth. Just because we don't see it—yet!—doesn't mean it isn't happening, just around the corner, just past the bend in the road, just out of visibility to our human, earth-bound eye.

Just because we can't see God's work, doesn't mean God isn't at work. So we walk under the great domed ceiling of the world, gilded with sun and polished clouds and framed by the dark scrolling wood of tree branches, and lift our hands, and lift our voices, and sign our prayers, "Thanking you in advance..."

And try not to forget the vital closing,

"I am, very truly yours."

Just Wondering...

What if you start a thank-you list to God? As though you were writing God a thank you letter, preferably of course in cursive since that's also very good for the brain. During good times this is soul-opening; during difficult seasons this becomes a life-saving tool.

How do you feel about thanking God in advance for prayer answers that haven't actually materialized yet? Is it presumptuous or a faith venture? Why? What would it do for your spirit, to thank God in advance over your prayer list?

. . .

JOURNAL A FEW THOUGHTS about what it means to be "very truly yours" in terms of your relationship with God.

Dear God.
The day, or night, stretches long before me,
and my list stretches even longer.
Help me to trust that you are indeed doing new things,
all day long.
Sign me, very truly yours.
Because that is what I want to want, more than anything.
Amen.

DAY FIVE: A TABLE OF MISFITS

GUESTS OF DISTINCTION

> "Then the angel said to me,
> 'Write this: Blessed are those who are invited to
> the wedding supper of the Lamb!'"
> Rev. 19:9

Chairs scraped over old wooden floors. Voices rose, guests seated themselves with friends and family. Laughter and stories and interlaced histories wove together, creating a warm fabric of celebration. The tines of forks pinged against glasses in signal to the bride and groom, "Kiss! Kiss!"[1]

At Table Ten, nine of us assembled. We seemed to be a leftover group. A few extended relatives who didn't talk to one another but bickered and occasionally snuck away for a smoke on the patio. The oldest couple in the entire crowd, who were parents of friends of the couple. And me. A table of misfits. I grinned. Jesus' words chimed in my soul: "When someone invites you to a wedding feast, do not take the place of honor, for a person more distinguished than you may have been invited" (Luke 14:8). No problem there—I'd skidded into the table arrangement long after placards were embossed and seating configured.

Conversation crashed around us, but at our table, people slumped in awkward silence. I'd planted myself near the elderly couple, who turned out to be hard of hearing.

We craned our necks and peered through the battered railing to glimpse the newlyweds at their elevated head table. Toasts and speeches, jokes and age-old stories brought chuckles and tears. After getting a crick from looking around a pillar, I turned to observe the strangers at my table, prepared to start from scratch in the "getting to know you for the next uncomfortable ninety minutes" portion of the festivities.

How on earth did I find myself seated at the splintery table on rickety chairs with people I had never seen in my life?

The night before, at the wedding rehearsal, the bride and groom invited me—or maybe I was the last person standing in the cramped quarters—to sit with them at their table for the rehearsal dinner. I knew exactly no one else in the entire noisy room. If only I'd said before the menus arrived, "Thank you so very much, but I need to scoot." Long drive, it's late, big day tomorrow, etc. But no. In a burst of collegiality and unusual extroversion, I said yes, and we shared a conversationally-stunted meal. That allowed me to dread the wedding dinner for only 24 hours.

I absolutely love weddings—as part of the crew that creates the ceremony, as one who comes alongside the couple and offers friendship, counsel, marriage and relationship tools. I love every bit of that. And I actually love people, too. Their stories, their hopes. I love to listen, to ask questions. I love all that.

But in the din of the banquet hall, focus presented a challenge in listening to individuals.

Fortunately, no one spoke at our table, resolving that problem. I figured I could focus just fine, and turned to the eldest couple, pulling their stories from them. Such a treasury of anecdotes and wisdom they'd amassed in their 160 combined years on the planet.

I glanced around Table Ten. We represented nearly a thousand years of living. None of us fit at the wedding table, yet we were all invited to the wedding. A table of misfits, with one element in common. We loved the bride and groom. We were each invited to the celebration because they loved us.

Then, I remembered.

> Let us rejoice and be glad
>   and give him glory!
>   For the wedding of the Lamb has come,
>   and his bride has made herself ready.
>   Fine linen, bright and clean,
>   was given her to wear."
>
> Then the angel said to me, 'Write this: Blessed are those who are invited to the wedding supper of the Lamb!' (Rev. 19:7-9)

The wedding feast of the Lamb. Where none of us match but where we are deeply loved. A table of misfits at the ultimate matrimonial feast.

I can hardly wait.

. . .

Just Wondering...

How do you feel about parties? Run from them, or run to them? How is it different if you don't know the people there? When do you feel like a misfit?

My own judgmental attitude often separates me from others. Or my fear of "different" and not being able to find a common denominator. Both are hugely problematic in our world, and I'm surprised to find these attitudes lurking in my soul. How about you?

What's the common denominator between you and others you meet for the first time? How do you bridge the differences? When you consider the "wedding supper of the Lamb," who do you hope will be there? How will your life and actions help that occur?

Dear Lord Jesus!
You've invited me to the wedding feast,
and there I will meet so many people and none of us match
but all of us love you, and are loved.
Please allow me to love others toward you,
so we can sit at table together on that great day.
Amen.

WEEKEND SIX SEGUE

BRIDGING TO TOMORROW

In your journal, write about some of the places where you've experienced God's presence this week, and how that has impacted you, your day, your soul, your relationships. Taking time to notice takes away some of our strained isolation and counteracts the feelings of abandonment so common during hard times. God *is* a very present help to us. We just don't always notice.

Where did you lose that sense that God was present to you? Or lose your bearings (or your mind, even just a fraction)? At the end of a day, or week, tracking back through our encounters for loss of presence, for places where we've been off-center, allows us to redirect. Remember that time when you blew up? What were you really hoping for, deep down, in that instance?

When we can notice, get clear, and get forgiven, we find increasing freedom. It's a shortcut out of shame, something I love to imagine eliminating more efficiently.

Examining our days for God's closeness, and our getting

off track, is part of an ancient practice called *Examen*. What a gift, to live. Really, really live, regardless of external circumstances.

The great freedom of being so wildly, crazily loved, of living into the great good news and the peace of Jesus, is that then we become a bridge, too. Our very lives beckon others into a life that will never die.

That's quite a headline.

SCRIPTURES FOR THE WEEK, to review and meditate upon using Lectio Divina, journaling or another method:

"Greater love has no one than this: to lay down one's life for one's friends."
John 15:13

"Behold, I bring you good news of great joy which will be for all the people."
Luke 2:10 NAS

"The peace of God, which transcends all understanding, will guard your hearts and your minds in Christ Jesus."
Philippians 4:7

"Behold, I am doing a new thing; now it springs forth, do you not perceive it?"

Is. 43:19 ESV

"Then the angel said to me,
'Write this: Blessed are those who are invited to the wedding supper of the Lamb!'"
Rev. 19:9

CLOSING WORD

Carrying the Light Forward

As we exit our time together, I feel a sense of "I will miss you so much!" that comes from spending time with a friend. My journey has been made better because of people who cared enough about me to pour wisdom, hope, and challenge into my life. People who have spoken good news, great love, and the gift of forgiveness. Friends who've invited me to view life through the lens of anticipation, to watch for God's "new things" in this world. People who have loved me enough to invite me to the wedding supper of the Lamb.

Would you consider taking this book, and meeting with a friend who needs a companion on the way? Particularly now, as we skid through perhaps the hardest season any of us can remember, loneliness and regret will threaten to tag along and nip our ankles. Mistakes will toggle our shame button. The sheer economics of our life will have shifted, and fear will want to squeeze our heart into contortions.

We are stronger together, and it continues to be true: it is not good to be alone. Thank you for the honor of this traveling, for trusting enough to move out of darkness and into light with me, and gazing into the eyes of the One who is crazy about us.

Need more proof? Here's what God told the wayward Israelites, in Jeremiah 31.

"They found grace out in the desert, these people who survived the killing. Israel, out looking for a place to rest, met God out looking for them!" God told them, "I've never quit loving you and never will. Expect love, love, and more love! And so now I'll start over with you and build you up again, dear virgin Israel. You'll resume your singing, grabbing tambourines and joining the dance." (Jeremiah 31:2-4, The Message)

CAN'T WAIT to see you at the Wedding of the Lamb. Until then, let's practice our dance steps and expect love, love, and more love. From God, through us, and into the world.

It's just...brilliant.

ABOUT JANE RUBIETTA

HUMOR. HOPE. HELP. GOOD FOR THE HEART.

Jane Rubietta writes in planes, trains, and automobiles, and prays there, too. She draws people into God's heart and purpose. She is dramatic, joyful, fun, and honest. Her speaking and preaching are practical, personal, and often hilarious. Jane has spoken for churches, districts, and national leadership around the continent and the globe.

Jane is married to her best friend, Rev. Rich Rubietta. They co-lead Abounding Ministries, a not-for-profit inviting people of all ages into God's life-changing love. They bring hope, laughter, values, and music into schools, retreats, worship services, conventions, and camps.

A prolific author, Jane has written hundreds of articles for a wide range of publications. Her twenty-one books include her critically acclaimed debut novel, *The Forgotten Life of Evelyn Lewis,* as well as *Worry Less, Live More, Heartbeat of a Mother,* and *Quiet Places,* all featured on international Reading Programs. She attended Trinity Divinity School and Indiana

University School of Business, and is passionate about helping people live into God's dreams for them.

All of Jane's books are designed for use in small groups, and she'd love to meet you over a video-chat with your group.

NEED A LITTLE HELP, Hope and Humor?

CONTACT JANE about speaking for your convention, conference, retreat, or group. She speaks internationally, and absolutely loves helping people laugh, learn, and live their best life. She's also available for video-training and conferences.

MORE INFO at JaneRubietta.com or email her at Jane@JaneRubietta.com

READY TO WRITE? Want to Start a Speaking Ministry?

JANE HAS HELPED LITERALLY hundreds of people build writing and speaking platforms as they live into their calling and the deep longing on their hearts. If you're not sure how to get started, or you've tried and quit, or you're ready for the next step in your ministry of words, reach out to her. You won't be sorry. Unless you don't take the next step!

For more info, visit LifeLaunchMe.com or email Jane@LifeLaunchMe.com

NOTES

DAY ONE: JOB DESCRIPTION

1. First appeared in *indeed,* April 20-21, 2019, p. 51-52.

DAY TWO: THE PERFECT GIFT

1. First appeared in *indeed,* March 1, 2009, p. 2-3.

DAY THREE: ALTARING WORRY

1. First appeared in *indeed,* March 19-20, 2016, p. 20-21.

DAY FIVE: TWIRLING IN CHURCH

1. First appeared in *indeed,* July 7-8, 2012, p. 8-9.

DAY TWO: SIGHTED

1. First appeared in *indeed,* July 6-7, 2019, p. 7-8.

DAY THREE: #FAIL

1. First appeared in *indeed,* March 31-April 1, 2018, p. 32-33.

DAY FOUR: BOOTS ON THE GROUND

1. First appeared in *indeed,* March 11-12, 2017, p. 12-13.

DAY FIVE: TRAINING FOR THE HIGH SEAS

1. First appeared in *indeed,* January 14-15, 2017, p. 16-17.
2. Guthrie, Woody. "Roll On Columbia." Words by Woody Guthrie, Music based on "Goodnight, Irene" (Huddie Ledbetter and John Lomax) © Copyright 1936 (renewed), 1957 (renewed) and 1963 (renewed) by Woody Guthrie Publications, Inc. & TRO-Ludlow Music, Inc. (BMI)

WEEKEND TWO SEGUE

1. Frederick Buechner, *Beyond Words: Daily Readings in the ABCs of Faith* (NY: HarperCollins, 2004), p. 118.

DAY ONE: STEP OUT OF THE TRAFFIC

1. *Indeed,* July 11-12, 2010, p. 11-12.

DAY TWO: THE ENDLESS SONG

1. First appeared in *indeed,* November 4-5, 2006, p. 11-12.

DAY THREE: RESCUED FROM A RED-LIGHT PAST

1. First appeared in *indeed,* March 10-11, 2007 p. 11-12.
2. There is some question as to whether Rahab was actually an innkeeper or innkeeper's daughter, rather than a prostitute.

DAY FOUR: KLIEG LIGHTS

1. First appeared in *indeed,* March 1-2, 2008, p. 203.

DAY FIVE: SAVING LIVES

1. First appeared in *indeed,* July 1, 2018, p. 3-4.

DAY ONE: OFFSTAGE VIEW

1. First appeared in *indeed,* July 11-12, 2009, p. 12-14.

DAY TWO: IT'S IMPOSSIBLE

1. First appeared in *indeed,* January 1, 2006, p. 8-9.

DAY THREE: WALKING THE LINE

1. First appeared in *indeed,* January 13-14, 2007.

DAY FOUR: YAKETY YAK

1. First appeared in *indeed,* January 5-6, 2008, p. 6-7.

DAY FIVE: ACTIVATING DYNAMITE

1. First appeared in *indeed,* September 1, 2019, p. 2-3.
2. One could transliterate the word as DYNAMIS but the more accurate transliteration is DUNAMIS.

DAY ONE: I ONCE WAS BLIND

1. First appeared in *indeed,* July 16-17, 2011, p. 16-17.

DAY TWO: LOOKING FOR ANSWERS

1. First appeared in *indeed,* September 8-9, 2018, p. 9-10.

DAY THREE: FROM FEAR TO FASTING

1. First appeared in *indeed,* July 2-3, 2005.

DAY FOUR: PACK RAT

1. First appeared in *indeed,* August 18-19, 2007, p. 48-49.
2. https://www.alzu.org/blog/2014/12/30/questions-for-caregivers-about-a-loved-one-with-alzheimers-disease-is-it-normal-clutter-or-hoarding/ Accessed 4/13/20.

DAY FIVE: CLOSE ENCOUNTERS OF THE HEALING KIND

1. First appeared in *indeed,* July 9-10, 2016, p. 10-11.

DAY ONE: THE BRIDGE

1. First appeared in *indeed,* January 5-6, 2019, p. 67.
2. BBC News, October 3, 2018 https://www.bbc.com/news/uk-45732361 accessed October 5, 2018; April 20, 2020.

DAY TWO: R.S.V.P AND A.S.A.P.

1. First appeared in *indeed,* December 16-17, 2017, p. 46-47.

DAY THREE: THINKING CAP

1. First appeared in *indeed,* Mary 5-6, 2018, p. 6-7.

DAY FOUR: THANKING YOU IN ADVANCE

1. First appeared in *indeed,* January 13-14, 2018, p. 14-16.

DAY FIVE: A TABLE OF MISFITS

1. First appeared in *indeed,* May 4-5, 2019, p. 5-6.

www.ingramcontent.com/pod-product-compliance
Lightning Source LLC
Chambersburg PA
CBHW071347080526
44587CB00017B/3007